END-TIME LIVING

END-TIME LIVING

Despite Conflict and Hardship, All Is Well

DAVID S. HEEREN

End-Time Living
Copyright © 2021 by David S. Heeren. All rights reserved.

No part of this publication may be reproduced, stored in a retrieval system or transmitted in any way by any means, electronic, mechanical, photocopy, recording or otherwise without the prior permission of the author except as provided by USA copyright law.

The opinions expressed by the author are not necessarily those of URLink Print and Media.

1603 Capitol Ave., Suite 310 Cheyenne, Wyoming USA 82001
1-888-980-6523 | admin@urlinkpublishing.com

URLink Print and Media is committed to excellence in the publishing industry.

Book design copyright © 2021 by URLink Print and Media. All rights reserved.

Published in the United States of America

Library of Congress Control Number: 2021915365
ISBN 978-1-64753-895-8 (Paperback)
ISBN 978-1-64753-896-5 (Digital)

23.07.21

CONTENTS

Foreword 7

Chapter 1: A Visit to Schaeffer's World 11

Chapter 2: Keepers of the Watch 24

Chapter 3: Let Us Pray for the U.S.A. 46

Chapter 4: Prepare and Share 60

Chapter 5: Firm and Fearless 67

Chapter 6: Moral Dissipation...............................74

Chapter 7: Trusting a Trustworthy God.............81

Chapter 8: The Song of Songs..............................90

Final Word 125

FOREWORD

'ALL IS WELL'...BUT IS IT REALLY?

Theme of this book is a Christian lifestyle that will produce fulfillment and joy even under the prophesied duress of the end-time. The sermon of Jesus occupying the most Bible space is about this topic. His second longest, though not exclusively about the end-time, also adheres to this theme. Both sermons were delivered by the Lord to crowds that had gathered on mountainsides.

Three key words in the subtitle of this book, *All Is Well*, do not appear at first to be fit for Christian material that emphasizes coping with the end-time challenges described by Jesus in Matthew chapter 24. It is a perfect fit, however, for the first of his two great sermons, which begins with the opening of the fifth chapter of the same biblical book.

In the first 12 verses of Matthew chapter five, Jesus described nine progressive ways for Christians to obtain blessedness, which in this context appears to be a synonym for Christian joy. I call it progressive because the language of Jesus indicates that more blessedness is achieved by adopting the lifestyle described in the final two statements of his about blessedness than the first seven. This is true even though the first is about humility, which we can easily visualize as a blessed state of being in contrast to the last two about persecution.

He said "Blessed are those who are persecuted because of righteousness, for theirs is the kingdom of heaven. Blessed are you when people insult you, persecute you and falsely say all kinds of evil against you because of me. Rejoice and be glad, because great is your reward in heaven, for in the same way they persecuted the prophets who were before you." (Mat. 5:10-12)

The first few times I read this, it didn't make sense to me. But now I think I understand.

When was Peter most blessed? Was it when he avoided persecution and perhaps even death by fleeing from the mob that was intent upon crucifying Jesus? Or when less than two months later, after much repentant prayer, he spoke about Jesus, without a microphone, in a voice so powerful that it could be heard by multitudes on the streets of Jerusalem?

And three-thousand people entered the kingdom of God.

There is consistency throughout the Bible, of the Lord blessing believers who stand firm in the face of persecution and participate in the conversion of others. This is why Jesus refers to persecution as the most blessed of the nine beatitudes. It pleases Him more when His people stand strong and courageous while facing grave peril than when they run for their lives.

No matter what we have to endure during the tribulation that Jesus prophesied for "all nations," no matter how bad things get (and they aren't great right now), we will be most blessed and, indeed, for us all we be well, if we can stand firm for Him until the end. (Mat. 24:13-14).

The phrase *stand firm* is used often in the Bible, and it isn't just a physical stance. Paul wrote that believers should "stand firm in one spirit, contending as one man for the faith of the gospel without being frightened in any way by those who oppose you." (Phil. 1:27-28)

Whatever courses our personal paths take, we know from the prophecies of Jesus, Joel, Zechariah, Isaiah, and others that during the end-time millions of people will be saved from sin and its hellish destination, and gain entrance into the kingdom of heaven. The Lord had in mind saving people, physically and spiritually, as evidenced by these words from the patriarch Joseph to his jealous brothers near the end of the book of Genesis:

"You intended to harm me, but God intended it for good to accomplish the saving of many lives. So don't be afraid. I will provide for you and your children." (Gen. 50:20)

Joseph's statement contained a promise for his once-treacherous brothers, which he then turned into reality. Believers today have comparable assurance from this biblical statement: "We know that in all things God works for the good of those who love him, who have been called according to his purpose." (Romans 8:28)

David S. Heeren

CHAPTER ONE

A VISIT TO SCHAEFFER'S WORLD

In 1976, year of the bicentennial celebration of the United States, Christian scholar Francis A. Schaeffer wrote a book suggesting that the U.S.A. was within a decade of demise. That book, *How Should we then Live,* discussed the atrophy of the U.S.A. and other free nations of the Western Hemisphere. Schaeffer zeroed in on Russia, leader of a socialist empire known as The Soviet Union, as the likely survivor of the struggle with what he thought to be a weakening western civilization.

One of Schaeffer's observations was that Western Hemisphere Christianity had lost much of its strength. Another concern of his was escalating inflation boding potential economic collapse. He believed the spiritually and economically- weakened U.S.A. would be unable to survive beyond 1986.

Schaeffer wrote: "Wherever Marxist-Leninism has had power, it has at no place in history shown where it has not brought forth oppression. As soon as

(Communists) have had the power, the desire of the majority has become a concept without meaning."[1]

But how was Schaeffer to know that nearly a half-century of leftist-leaning American presidents in both political parties would end in 1980, with a man, Ronald Reagan, who was a committed Christian and a dedicated foe of imperialistic Marxism?

Reagan referred more than once to the Soviet Union as the "evil empire." By cutting off the wheat supply that had been donated annually to the Russian Communists by previous U.S. administrations, Reagan placed pressure on the unstable Soviet economy.

The Soviet Union collapsed in 1987, while Reagan was president. It was disbanded in 1991 after he had left office. But today, 30 years later, the U.S.A. finds itself back at a similar vulnerable place to where it was when Schaeffer was writing his book.

Only now, Russia is headed by a new group of Communists with the same aspirations of Nikita Khrushchev, who told us, "We will bury you!" And we find ourselves in the U.S.A. dominated by a political party headed by men, including that party's last three presidents, who have given great concessions to a larger and stronger group of Communists, the Chinese, whose nation has nearly five times the population of the U.S.A.

---

[1] Francis A. Schaeffer, *How Should we then Live?*, 1976, p. 215.

We are in deep trouble politically, morally and spiritually.

The behavior of thieves and liars is displeasing to God, according to the Bible. But, if anything, today these are even more pervasive and this nation appears worse off than it was in 1976.

Read this to patriotic Americans who were forced to abide a crime spree masquerading as a presidential election in 2020, and you'll see most of them nod their heads. It's a reason for reading this book, which contains information that could lead to life-saving behavior during the end-time difficulties prophesied by Jesus and other biblical writers.

The best recourse remaining for the U.S.A. is the humbly repentant prayers of God's remnant. A pertinent Bible promise is 2 Chronicles 7:14: "If my people who are called by my name will humble themselves, and pray, and seek my face, and turn from their wicked ways, then I will hear from heaven, forgive their sin, and heal their land."

Trouble with this is that most of the time, when I hear this text quoted, the references to *sin* and *wicked ways* are omitted. We cannot afford to pretend that evil behavior does not exist in our homeland, or in ourselves.

Fraudulent elections are not new phenomena here. They are simply a much bigger problem now than 61 years ago when a presidential candidate benefited, perhaps decisively, from the once-infamous-but-now-almost-forgotten votes of dead people in the Chicago area.

Or 21 years ago when a presidential candidate got aid from a high court that decided a recount in Florida should be limited to the three most extreme leftist counties out of the 67 in the state. The other 64 apparently were unrecognizable to the judges because they were excluded from the process. Also discounted were the votes of Florida's military personnel. Talk about ignoring the constitution!

As this is being written, in winter of 2021, we have recently completed a four-year term during which two-dozen attempts reportedly were made to murder the president of the United States. This may seem like just a statistic until it is recognized as fact that the 44 previous presidents, in total, were not confronted by potential assassins that many times.

In 2020, some extreme-left politicians holding high office, including state governors and city mayors, ordered police not to intervene while organized rioters looted and burned downtown areas of their cities with little or no resistance and no fear of being arrested. Police who did try to enforce local laws drew gunfire that killed many of them.

The "major media" as a group apparently had different opinions from the general public about what constituted an important news story because, to my knowledge, they failed to report nationwide any presidential assassination attempts or any murders of police officers other than one for which they placed blame erroneously.

This partisan cover-up of murder and attempted murder represented one of hundreds of times during my lifetime that the media proved unreliable. By this time, the head-scratching question has become: Why does anyone pay attention to them anymore?

I was a professional journalist for nearly 50 years. It was because of personal contact with liars in my profession that I stopped watching TV news more than 40 years ago. Subsequent events have reinforced the TV-set-off decision to the present day.

Now infamous media lies were rehashed to absurdity concerning a violent incident on Jan. 6, 2021, for which talking heads placed false blame. TV reporting of this riot included not only false accusations, but also omission of information identifying the actual perpetrators.

Because of law changes favoring the media to the extent that it is almost impossible to succeed in a lawsuit against them, they are free to say what they please, and that means telling lies or at the very least leaning to the left in every important story. Here's a response that will work about 99% of the time:

If the "major media" are in league in reporting a story almost identically, listeners should do these things: 1. Write down in detail the media position; 2. Write the word *innocent* next to names of persons they are accusing of guilt; 3. Write the newscasters names as guilty (of lying); 4. Write as guilty the names of political allies and so-called witnesses they have interviewed in order to lend support to their false position; 5. In the case of partisan political accusations, write down as innocent those politicians they accuse of guilt; 6. Write down as guilty those they are using as witnesses to the alleged guilt of the innocent ones; 7. Write down the crimes and/or immoral acts involved and next to those the names of all politicians participating in the accusations.

Do these things, and you will hardly ever be wrong. Nearly all accusations emanating from the left are about immoral and/or illegal things that many of them are familiar with because they have been guilty of them.

Finally, ask yourself this question: Why am I watching and/or listening to liars? If everyone who is aware of the lying would turn off their TV sets, the liars would lose advertising support and be forced off the air.

Through the years they have become bolder. Not long ago there was a well-publicized report in which several of them not only admitted they were all members of the same political party, but also confessed publicly that the cause of socialism was so important to them that they were willing to lie about anything they thought would assist its advancement toward totalitarianism. They made these comments in public. It's no secret any more.

They are committed to lying.

This is a good place for a factual interjection. Those calling themselves progressives or liberals or socialists are actually Marxists. Since Marxism is the basis for both kinds of extant socialism, Communism and Nazism, and nothing else, they must be either Communists or Nazis. None of them, to my knowledge, will admit to being Nazis. Ergo, you tell me, what are they?

Ultimate goal of international socialism/communism, as outlined by its primary founder Karl Marx, and understood by Putin, Xi Jinping (China) and other current Communist dictators, is to rule the world. One of their primary goals today is to bring about economic collapse followed by revolution destroying the republic government (it's not a democracy) of the United States. The U.S.A. seems to be the last line of defense for freedom-loving people, but it isn't strong any more.

We need to keep this in mind as the course of this book unfolds.

Crime Today? That's OK

During my long tenure in the media, I got to know every trick of the Marxists. I knew them as long ago as when they began plotting with radical educators to rewrite American history books. They called it *historical revisionism*. And they succeeded. There are many purposeful untruths in the American history books being used today in public school systems.

Another trait of theirs that I learned very early was that if a popular Marxist was a criminal, they deemed it okay for him to hold high office. One of them was elected to the House of Representatives after serving a prison term for a felony while I was a young journalist in Broward County, FL, He was re-elected so many times I lost count. I discussed this with a left-wing journalist and he nodded his okay for felons agreeing with his politics to hold congressional seats.

After the debacle called a vote recount in 2000, when I suggested that the election supervisor in Palm Beach County, where I was working at the time, should be fired, I was confronted by horrified newsroom reactions.

Yes, she broke laws in trying her best to get together enough bogus votes to reverse the outcome of the election. The scandal was so bad that Rush Limbaugh drew laughs for years with his sarcastic comments about "hanging chads." But she was associated with the Marxists. And it was unthinkable to them even to consider firing a prominent Marxist no matter what she had done.

To them, the opposite principle prevailed for the other political party. Instead of even-if-guilty-we-don't-care, it was guilty-even-after-being-proved-innocent. Years later it was the most obvious victim of the execution of this philosophy who finally began calling their reporting "fake news."

False accusations against innocent people were among the things prophesied by Jesus to become prevalent during the end-time. He said that the false accusers against Christians would include family members (Luke 21:16).

He also said: "Blessed are you when people insult you, persecute you and falsely say all kinds of evil against you because of me. Rejoice and be glad, because great is your reward in heaven, for in the same way they persecuted the prophets who were before you." (Mat. 5:11-12)

The great number of murders of police officers and the record-setting attempts to take the life of a president, described above, are indicators that we have now, indeed, entered the era described by the Bible as the end-time. And no matter how bad things look right now, for us it should be an occasion of rejoicing in the Lord. We should be happy and hopeful because we are headed for a victorious finale, the Second Coming of Jesus, which will be a cause of celebration to millions upon millions of people who will meet him in the air.

Now that we appear to be within the end-time period, it is important for us also to be watchful. This was the thing mentioned most often in Jesus' end-time sermon. It is only by being watchful – alert to what is taking place and able to discern its implications – that we will spiritually thrive as did Jesus' faithful first-century followers.

Fellow Americans, we are in trouble because we have not been watchful as Jesus described it. This includes seeing the threat of evil and doing something about it. In my case, I saw but did nothing about developing political corruption in Broward County. And, apparently, no one else did anything about it, either.

What happened? That corruption was manifest in the 2016 presidential election when Broward County's election supervisor and political associates of hers locked themselves in a room for several days, after Election Day, filling out bogus ballots for their favored candidate in hopes that they could lift her from defeat to victory.

They failed, but their successors in counties throughout the U.S.A. succeeded with the same tactic in the 2020 election. Statistical analysis has proven that they filled out millions of phony ballots and even used rigged voting machines to change votes cast for one candidate to the credit of the other candidate.

Concerted prayers by serious Christians could be a starting point for the spiritual effort needed to stave off full-scale Communist revolution. But can we build prayer-based revival out of the ashes of faith all around us?

According to one estimate, fifty percent of the churches that were fully operational in January of 2020 no longer were in December. The pulpits of most had been vacated.

During the years of my lifetime, Christianity in the U.S.A. has become endangered. Young people being taught in public schools that there is no God and receiving little or no contradiction of that statement from parents, have flocked into the camp of atheistic socialism.

D. James Kennedy said 15 years ago that he had determined through his international ministry, Evangelism Explosion, that less than half of the Christian pastors in the U.S.A. were actually believers. He said the percentage of so-called Christian laymen with faith described in the Bible as being born-again was less than that of the unbelieving pastors.

Those numbers have been declining for as long as I can remember and are probably lower now.

The church is even weaker in Europe than the U.S.A. Other than a few prosperous mission areas, it is practically non-existent in large parts of Asia and Africa. Weak faith is always reflected by absence of Bibles for believers to read and/or poor understanding of that greatest of books. And so it should come as no surprise to us that indifferent believers have changed the word *trespasses* (sins) to *debts* in the now official version of the Lord's Prayer.

Is there anyone out there who wouldn't want to have his/her debts forgiven? But sin: Most people, apparently even Christians who should be the first to admit their fallibility, don't want to talk about sin. Or even to admit that such a thing exists. These dubious believers, including many in positions of leadership, are altering, through the omission of "sin" and "wicked ways," the great biblical revival verse: 2 Chronicles 7:14.

Revival is what we need. We must start with an understanding of what revival is. There are probably as many professing Christians who misunderstand the basics of revival as there are those who claim to be born-again without knowing what the term means. (John 3:3, 16).

We need to begin with re-establishment of the biblical principle that all of us have sinned and fall short of the glory of God (Romans 3:23). If we do not humbly confess and repent of known sins, our nation, the United States of America, will reap devastation.

Millions must do this prayerfully, with determined repetition, before we can expect revival to happen. But if and when enough of us – however many it takes – repent and seek the face of God in fervent, persistent prayer, we will experience unprecedented revival as millions of unbelievers turn to the Lord.

This is what happened soon after Jesus was crucified, resurrected and taken to heaven. And, if we are obedient to do our part, we can be confident that, when Jesus returns, the end will be greater than was the beginning.

Concerning circumstances similar to those we now face, Schaeffer wrote: "If further recessions come, if fear of the loss of personal peace and prosperity increases, if wars and threats of wars intensify, if violence and terrorism spread, if food and other resources in the world become even scarcer – and all of these are more than possible – then the trend is speeded up. As these things come upon people who have only the values of personal peace and affluence, they will crush them as a six-wheeled truck will crush the little bridge."[2]

Purpose of this book is to provide each of us with the kind of spiritual resources necessary to apply brakes to that truck.

---

[2] Ibid, p. 252.

CHAPTER TWO

KEEPERS OF THE WATCH

Not only did the three Gospel writers all begin their accounts of Jesus' sermon with the same word, but in total they mentioned watchfulness twelve times. Nothing else of sufficient importance to be considered keys for Christian living during the end time was mentioned by our Lord more than three times.

A person on watch must strive to keep awake. The word implies vigilant purpose. A night watchman, for example, does his protective work at night and sleeps during the day.

He must stay awake and aware of what is going on all around him. He must not allow an enemy to encroach on the territory he is protecting, whether it is a beloved family, a city wall or a store that is selling valuable commodities.

The first time Jesus mentioned the word *watch* in his sermon the rest of the sentence was about avoiding deception. Satan, foremost enemy of God, is referred to in the Bible as the father of lies (John 8:44). His demonic underlings are spiritual clones for their dishonest leader.

Just as the devil's first recorded lie was for the purpose of deceiving a human being (Eve), most of his work today begins and ends with dishonesty. This is evident in the U.S.A. beneath the umbrellas of politics, media, education and entertainment. I overheard many vicious lies after becoming a journalist six decades ago. Today, the lying is even worse than it was then.

Christians should seek honest sources of information, such as *The Epoch Times* and Christian publications. We should avoid everything emphasized by the "major" media and their cohorts in politics, public education and entertainment, if we want to be obedient to God by avoiding deception.

Media deception is the worst because we expect the truth to be told on so-called newscasts. All of us are aware that truth takes a backseat to partisanship in politics. The same is true with entertainers, most of whom make no secret of their alliance with leftist causes and, also, with the new prevalence of radicalism in all phases of public education.

There is a simple way to avoid media deception, which of course includes interviews with "friends" in the other three fields. The way I avoid the entire package is simply to refuse to read any so-called "major" newspapers or news magazines, and to refuse to turn my TV set to any newscast at all (no, not even Fox).

My TV set has not been tuned to a major network for anything, even a leftist-slanted comedy or dramatic show, in ten years. I have not watched a network news program in at least forty years. All of these have become corrupted in more ways than one.

But the worst thing of all is the blatant lies that are now told about nearly everybody and everything that doesn't gibe with socialism. And in a republic such as the U.S.A., this covers just about everything.

Watchful Preparation

Although Jesus' first reference to watching had to do with avoiding deception, there was more. His next comment on the subject concerned His own Second Coming. He said we should be watchful, that is, alert, so that we could be prepared, not surprised, since we cannot know the day or hour of that event (Mat. 24:42-44)

Study of the 24th chapter of Matthew and the 21st chapter of Luke helps with this. Within those contexts we learn these details about visible celestial activity related to the "sign" of Jesus' Second Coming and events preceding His return:

- Solar and lunar eclipses appear concurrently. (Mat. 24:29)
- Moon's light weakens even when not eclipsed. (Mat. 24:29)

- Brilliant light flashes from horizon to horizon. (Mat. 24:27)
- "Stars fall." (Mat. 24:29)
- Celestial objects appear to be shaking. (Luke 21:26)
- Sea and waves roar. (Luke 21:25)
- Human beings become terrified. (Luke 21:26)

A comet is the only celestial object known to astronomers at this time that, if it is indeed the prophesied sign of the event, would be capable of fulfilling all of these qualifications. In fact, it is the only thing capable of fulfilling more than three of the seven.

Moreover, even though an asteroid does cause three of them, these are not comparable to the vast power unleashed by a comet. This was demonstrated in 1994 by an event on the surface of Jupiter. A comet that had been orbiting our solar system's largest planet for at least 20 years, began breaking apart. Its 22 pieces fell to the planet's surface over a period of about two weeks and the pieces exploded. Some of the explosions were of such enormity that a single one of them, transferred from Jupiter to earth, might have depopulated our planet.

Asteroids have no explosive potential whatsoever.

In order for the biblically prophesied end-time events to take place, the sign would have to be an object (or objects) that approach the earth, even perhaps colliding with this planet or dumping explosive objects onto its surface.

Besides a comet, the only other currently known possibilities for the celestial sign of Jesus' return, as He himself described it, are solar eclipse, lunar eclipse, concurrent solar and lunar eclipses, meteor(s), meteorite shower and asteroid. None of these would be even remotely comparable to a comet in danger presented to earth. Next in line, as we have mentioned, would be an asteroid.

We have mentioned that asteroids have no explosive contents, but there is another important difference between them and comets. Comets are enormous, with visible size that may be comparable to the sun and tails extending through space for millions of miles; asteroids, even those considered large, are comparable in surface area to a college campus. They are measured in meters, not millions of miles. They are not potential earth-destroyers.

Knowing the sign of Jesus' return and becoming watchful for it are important. There is a detailed discussion of it in my book *The High Sign*. There is also a clear summation of this subject in *Day of the Lord*.

The sign will need our focus of attention when it appears, so we can recognize it and fearlessly seek opportunities for sharing the Gospel during the interval of time we have to do so.

Stunned unbelievers will react to the celestial fireworks with terror. The ears of many will be open to hearing the Gospel message.

The last-chance salvation of unbelievers will be the final great victory of our Lord. There are many end-time salvation scriptures, but these are a few that I like from the Old Testament.:

Multitudes who sleep in the dust of the earth shall awake: some to everlasting life, others to shame and everlasting contempt. Those who are wise will shine like the brightness of the heavens, and those who lead many to righteousness like the stars forever and ever. (Dan. 12:2-3)

Multitudes, multitudes in the valley of decision! For the day of the Lord is near in the valley of decision. (Joel 3:14)

"In the whole land (world)," declares the Lord, "two-thirds will be struck down and perish; yet one-third will be left in it. This third I will put into the fire. I will refine them like silver and test them like gold. They will call on my name and I will answer them: I will say, 'They are my people.' And they will say, 'The Lord is our God.'" (Zech 13:8-9)

Final Word

The last words uttered by Jesus in his message about the end-time provide a good summation for us on the subject of watching: *"Be always on the watch, and pray that you may be able to escape all that is about to happen, and that you may be able to stand before the Son of Man." (Luke 21:36).*

There was a time when I wondered why Jesus placed more emphasis, at least in an end-time context, on watchfulness over prayerfulness. Comments following are explanatory.

According to Luke 21:36, watchfulness is an essential preliminary for acquiring the knowledge necessary for effective prayer. Prayer, in turn, is important for receiving guidance to avert evil so that we can stand firm before God and men (Mat. 24:13).

No wonder Jesus gave so much attention to the concept of watchfulness.

Being on watch, then, includes more than just what meets the eye. It also involves correct interpretation of everything that is going on around us. And this once again takes us all the way back to Eden where Eve was deceived about the genuineness of the source of the devil's lies and coaxed Adam into involvement.

I have heard it said that Adam was guiltier than Eve, because he recognized the devil's deception but went along with it, anyway, instead of lovingly correcting his mate.

It is not unusual for even a Christian to mistake lies coming from demonic sources for the absolute truth of the Lord. We must strive to maintain communion with God so as to avoid this kind of deception.

Prayer then is both the object for accomplishing communion with God and the avoidance of deception by the devil. But it cannot achieve maximum effectiveness without being undergirded by alert watchfulness.

The following excerpts from Luke's account of Jesus' end-time sermon contain topics worthy of being committed to prayer:

"Watch out that you are not deceived. For many will come in my name, claiming, 'I am he,' and 'The time is near.' Do not follow them." (Luke 21:8). This is a strong suggestion by Jesus for us to be watchful for attempts to deceive us and to reject them. It doesn't specifically mention prayer, but that should be the first thing we do.

"When you hear of wars and revolutions, do not be frightened. These things must happen first, but the end will not come right away." (Luke 21:9) The word *revolutions* appears only in Luke's account of Jesus' speech. It brings to mind the violence utilized by communists to gain control of susceptible nations. The thought of being tortured and/or murdered during a violent revolutionary coup is scary to most human beings. Jesus says simply, "Do not be frightened." Talk to him about it. He can handle it.

"There will be great earthquakes, famines and pestilences in various places, and fearful events and great signs from heaven." (Luke 21:11) Next introduced to this terrible scenario are natural disasters as deadly as wars and revolutions. It is obvious that Jesus does not want us to be fearful in any situation. With the world facing possible violent termination, I wonder if

I could be fearless without asking for and receiving help from the Lord.

"But before all this, they will lay hands on you and persecute you…This will result in your being witnesses to them. But make up your mind not to worry beforehand how you will defend yourself. For I will give you words and wisdom that none of your adversaries will be able to resist or contradict." (Luke 21:12-15) Prayer is essential. No one receives "words and wisdom" directly from God without asking for it. Our Christian witness isn't worth much without His input. And we cannot expect, without praying for it, to be able to speak calmly and persuasively to enemies capable of killing us.

Vigilant Watchfulness

The following are aspects of vigilant watchfulness cited in *The New Thayer's Greek Lexicon*:
1. To have been roused from sleep; to be awake.
2. To be cautious, active, give strict attention to.
3. To take heed lest through indolence some calamity occur.
4. To employ the most punctilious care in a thing.
5. Keep watch lest one be led to forsake Christ.
6. Keep watch lest one fall into sin.
7. Keep watch lest one be corrupted by errors.

Reading these enabled me to see for the first time how important Christian watchfulness is. According to the definitions of the cited Greek word, we must be spiritually alert in order to avoid disaster. We must pay attention. We must not become lazy or careless (indolent).

Watchmen were among the most important people in ancient cities. In Israel, the nights were divided into three watches. Each watchman upon a city's wall was responsible for reacting to any suspicious activity that might be associated with enemy attack during his watch.

If that happened, he was to blow his trumpet. The other watchmen would hear and sound their own trumpets awakening citizens throughout the city. The men would then arm themselves for battle.

The only things worse than a false alarm, to a watchman, were failing to sound the alarm because of falling asleep or losing vigilant attention long enough to allow enemy ingress that could result in disaster. A watchman guilty of sleeping or failing vigilance would be replaced on the city wall by someone else as soon as possible, that is, if the city was not by that time smoldering ashes.

Watchmen were not merely the most important protectors of a city. They became symbolic, spiritually, of believers in God who stood firm in faithfulness to Him no matter what hostility they faced from family members, fellow believers or outright enemies. They were vigilant for Christ no matter what.

If believers today become lethargic in their faith, it won't necessarily lead to forsaking Christ, but this could happen (No. 5). "Destructive calamity" (No. 3) is not something we should look forward to. Neither is falling into sin (No. 6), or being corrupted by errors (No. 7).

In my twenties, when I began work as a professional journalist. I overheard Marxist staff members of a large newspaper discussing a process they called "historical revisionism." Through this process they and their friends in public education intended to rewrite the history of the United States so that the good guys became bad guys and vice versa.

I did nothing about it; did not even pray that their efforts would be thwarted. Actually, I do not know of a single person who did anything about it.

And so, in public school textbooks today, we read many untruths concerning the history of the U.S.A. Contrary to books in current use, the truth is that nearly all slave-traders and slave-drivers were Democrats or were in the political lineage that was to become Democratic. It was Democrats who instigated the Civil War, the Ku Klux Klan and the assassination of President Lincoln.

Democrats later became active in "taking over" what now is known as the "major media," And so, from today's media, we hear blame for every bad thing and a lot of imaginary evil falsely falling upon the heads of just about everybody other than the guilty (themselves).

Democrats, original source of KKK racism in the U.S.A. now are vocal in calling nearly every white person other than themselves racists. They seem especially to enjoy accusing others of their own offenses.

An example of this was the repetitious accusation that former President Trump had colluded with Russia. No evidence has been found to this day in support of that accusation. In fact, even in the two politicized impeachment proceedings, no evidence of such collusion was presented.

However, 2016 presidential candidate Hillary Clinton made the mistake of allowing evidence to remain computer accessible that she colluded with Russia by selling to the still-Communist leadership of that nation a substance that could be used in making deadly weapons.

Bill Clinton, during his presidency, made a deal with Communist Chinese leaders to make China a "most favored nation" of the U.S.A. As we look around us in today, we see more products made in China than the U.S.A. Most of them are poor in quality. This is a problem threatening survival of the U.S.A.'s national economy with its unthinkable debt.

Moreover, current U.S. President Joe Biden and his son Hunter are well-known for building family wealth through collusion with the Chinese Communists. To put it simply, the U.S.A. has been losing business to China with the help of Democrat leaders, not Republicans, not Trump.

This is not about Democrats vs. Republicans, but about telling the truth in order to preserve the liberties we have in the United States. The Bible contains a multitude of verses admonishing liars.

If Republicans, instead of Democrats, were the untruthful ones, this would be all about them.

Christian Conservative Targets

Much of the media rancor has been piled undeservedly on the heads of Christian conservative constitutionalists and their heritage, including the first three presidents: George Washington, John Adams and Thomas Jefferson. In more recent times three other presidents have been prime candidates for media false accusation at least in part because of their Christian faith: Ronald Reagan, George W. Bush and the oft-targeted Trump.

To the Marxists, who have exploited an out-of-context Jefferson quote containing the words "separation of church and state" to justify action targeting Christian believers, existence of the misrepresented comment does not make him a good guy. Jefferson was not a deist, as they untruthfully assert, but a Christian who regularly exchanged correspondence concerning that faith with his friend, Adams.

While serving as superintendent of a large public school system, Jefferson required the placement of a Bible in the hands of every student. If someone did that today, he/she would be fired on the spot; indeed, one public school employee was fired recently after being seen praying on school property.

At no time did Jefferson say or even imply that he would exclude Christians from political office. To him, as he stated in the "separation of church and state letter" to a Christian leader that has been misused by Marxists to excuse their efforts to limit the political activity of Christians in the U.S.A., separation of church and state meant prohibiting politicians from meddling in church affairs, not vice-versa.

At this moment, after learning that vast numbers of the so-called millennial generation have accepted not only the lies they are reading in "revised" American history textbooks, but also in textbooks on other subjects, I feel remorse. I have asked the Lord to forgive me and to restore truth to public school textbooks or else move the hearts of Christians to educate their children in private or home schools.

None of this would be happening if God's people living in the U.S.A. had been watchful for potential evils, including historical revisionism of textbooks, and had prayed and taken action to prevent it.

At one time, more than a half-century ago, the atmosphere in this nation was conducive to eliminating dishonest voting and fact-altered public school textbooks. Today it is not.

It's partly my fault, but if memory serves, just about everyone I knew growing up was as indifferent to what was going on as was I.

We went along with the media hatred of Joe McCarthy, only to learn later to our dismay that McCarthy had been correct in identifying this nation's most urgent problem as the placement of Communists in prominent positions in what has come to be known as The Deep State.

Maybe we just didn't believe that anything so tragically evil could happen in our great nation. Why make a big deal out of an impossible event? Why even bother to watch out for it?

Biblical Faith Weakens

When I was young, predominant religious faiths in the U.S.A. were Christianity and Judaism. Today, biblical unbelief is weakening both faiths. But in fairness to the young, how can we expect them to join forces with Christians, if the believers of their acquaintance lack enthusiasm for the faith they profess?

We are in desperate need of spiritual revival. This revival must be based first of all on humble change of heart and mind. We must pray, earnestly seeking the intervention of God on our behalf. We must identify personal sins, confess them and resolve to put an end to them. And, equally important, we must adopt an attitude of determined watchfulness.

We must not allow ourselves to become so lethargic that we are easy victims for the unscrupulous.

Format for this strategy is found in 2 Chron. 7:14. This Bible verse is being highlighted in this book because it contains the precise formula for reversing the trend toward corruption in the U.S.A. If we do our fourfold part, God will hear from heaven, forgive our sins and heal out land.

Nominal Christians want to jump past the four personal requirements – especially the one about turning from wicked ways (repenting of sin). They want to proceed straight to the final promise that speaks of God healing the land. But He hasn't healed the land despite nearly a half-century of listening to these pleas.

I have vivid recollection of the great emphasis that was placed (verbally at least) on praying according to 2 Chron. 7:14 during national celebrations in 1976. It seems clear now that He is serious about waiting for us to meet the four requirements of that verse before fulfilling the three promises.

Most difficult of the four seems to be the final one. Believers refusing to acknowledge the parts of this Bible verse about turning from wicked ways and asking forgiveness for sin are unaware of the real problem or indifferent to it.

Any serious quest for national revival must begin right here, with confession and determination to eliminate or at least reduce personal sin. Much of this could be accomplished by simply doing as British Bible scholar Oswald Chambers often said: "Give up the right to yourself to Him."

Self-centeredness is the source of most sin.

If we continue indifferent about sinfulness, we are likely to see a continuance of the national decline that could lead, in the near future, to nationwide economic collapse and Marxist revolution. Communists have been successful in implementing the same plan in numerous nations.

The following conversation about revival is from Jonathan Cahn's book, *The Harbinger II, The Return*, a book in which the watchmen fall asleep:

"So as the week in which America was traumatized by the calamity of 9/11 came to its end, the word appointed for that moment was God's message to a nation traumatized by calamity. And what was that message? It was God calling that nation to return…and the promise that if they did return He would restore them that had failed, that had suffered catastrophe…and now God was calling it to return. And if the people returned, He would restore them."

"Return," I said. "In our first encounters, you focused on that word."

"And it was all there," he replied, "in the appointed scripture that followed 9/11. Behind the word return *or* turn *is the Hebrew word* shuv. *It also means to repent."*

"Repentance, the one thing missing after 9/11. America never returned because America never repented."

"Yes, and without repentance, there can be no return. And without return, there can be no revival and no restoration."

We walked slowly along the courtyard path, through the grass and the aged gravestones and under the trees that had not yet blossomed.

"Do you remember the scripture," he said, "that was joined to the ground of consecration, the word God gave Solomon to answer the prayers he had prayed at the dedication of the Temple?"

"Yes, the word appointed for the nation that had turned from God and suffered calamity, the calling to a fallen and wounded nation:

"If My people who are called by My name will humble themselves, and pray and seek My face, and turn from their wicked Ways, then I will hear from heaven, and will forgive their sin and heal their land." (2 Chron. 7:14)

Critical Role of Watchman

According to Francis A. Schaeffer, a good description of the critical role of a watchman during a troubled time comes from Ezekiel 33:1-11, 19. This part of the Bible yielded Schaeffer's book's title, *How Should We Then Live?* In that book, he used the King James Version of this text. We are using here the New International Version to quote from verses 1-6 and 10-11:

The word of the Lord came to me: "Son of man, speak to your countrymen and say to them: 'When I bring the sword against a land, and the people of the land choose one of their men and make him their watchman, then if anyone hears the trumpet but does not take warning and the sword comes and takes his life, his blood will be on his own head...If he had taken warning, he would have saved himself. But if the watchman sees the sword coming and does not blow the trumpet to warn the people and the sword comes and takes the life of one of them, that man will be taken away because of his sin, but I will hold the watchman accountable for his blood..."Son of man, say to the house of Israel, 'This is what you are saying: "Our offenses and sins weigh us down, and we are wasting away because of them. How then can we live?" Say to them, 'As surely as I live, declares the sovereign Lord, I take no pleasure in the death of the wicked, but rather that they turn from their ways and live.'"

Rewriting school textbooks to give validity to lies is not the only critical issue facing the U.S.A. today. Others include same-sex marriage, multi-gender sexuality, murder of unborn babies (abortion), exclusion of prayer and the Bible from public schools, and evidence of widespread corruption by prominent persons, including billionaires. Nations throughout the world have similar problems to ours.

Almost the entirety of the large-circulation media have become supporters of evil things. As I write this, pending in Congress is a horrific piece of legislation written in such a way as to be destructive of the constitutional rights of Christians to express their faith in public.

This bill is known as the Equality Bill, but, as often is the case with bills introduced by socialists, it is designed to have the effect of achieving the opposite of what its title implies. It is a big step toward achieving the Marxist goal of decimating the rights of believers as expressed in the U.S. Constitution and Bill of Rights as well as founding documents of all fifty states.

The role of spiritual watchmen in the U.S.A. has become vital, indeed. In the Case of the Equality Bill, the last recourse (and always the best one) is prayer. At this point, the situation appears next to hopeless, for leftists predominate everywhere in the nation's Capitol. At the moment, how they got there is unimportant. It's what they do while there that we must cope with.

Let's not stop with prayer against this bill. We have identified the evil opposition, and beyond watchfulness/participation how has God told us to respond? What should we do? Here's a comment by Jesus on the subject:

"You have heard that it was said, 'Love your neighbor and hate your enemy.' But I tell you: Love your enemies, and pray for those who persecute you, that you may be sons of your Father in heaven…If you love those who love you, what reward will you get? Are not even the tax collectors doing that? And if you greet only your brothers, what are you doing more than others? Do not even pagans do that?

Be perfect, therefore, as your heavenly Father is perfect."
(Mat. 5:43-48)

The greatest true story I have read about loving an enemy was accomplished by a 12-year-old boy, whose mother had been tortured until she died in a communist labor camp. Richard Wurmbrand, a Romanian believer who spent 12 years in communist detention centers, even though he had committed no crime, told this story in one of his books.

Wurmbrand wrote that the torturer wound up as a voluntary prisoner in the same prison camp where he had beaten to death the boy's mother. When he arrived there he told Wurmbrand that the boy had handed him a flower that he ordinarily would have given his mother on her birthday and said that he was giving it to him because she had told him to love everyone, even his enemies.

The repentant torture/murderer had tears in his eyes when he said to Wurmbrand: "I can't do it anymore."

He admitted that he broke emotionally after the boy gave him the flower. He then turned himself in to higher Communist authorities, asking to be removed from his position and placed in detention. He said he deserved to be there for what he had done.

The way God worked this out, the former torturer was at the right place at the right time to hear the Gospel from a man who was accustomed to sharing it, Richard Wurmbrand. He was also in the right frame of mind – deeply regretful of his sinful behavior – so that he could respond positively to the message and become a born-again Christian based on biblical texts, like this combination of two from the same book, that Wurmbrand shared with him:

God demonstrates his own love for us in this: While we were still sinners, Christ died for us…For the wages of sin is death, but the gift of God is eternal life in Christ Jesus our Lord. (Romans 5:8, 6:23)

Paul was setting an example for faithful Christians when he said he wanted to partake of the sufferings of Jesus: "I want to know Christ and the power of his resurrection and the fellowship of sharing in his sufferings, becoming like him in his death." (Phil. 3:10-11)

As for the boy whose loving act resulted in the salvation of his mother's murderer, according to Jesus, the boy's act of forgiving the murderer resulted in his own forgiveness: "For if you forgive men when they sin against you, your heavenly Father will also forgive you." (Mat 6:14)

Want to know why Jesus said we should love our enemies? This explains it.

CHAPTER THREE

LET US PRAY FOR THE U.S.A.

The themes below provide the basis for this book. However, except for watchfulness – the most often mentioned by Jesus in his end-time sermon, and theme of the previous chapter – they are not necessarily in order of frequency of usage by Jesus in his two mountainside sermons:

- Watch.
- Pray.
- Prepare for tough times.
- Share the Gospel.
- Stand firm, with head held high.
- Fear nothing, don't even worry.
- Be ready to flee and live off the land.
- Avoid moral dissipation.
- In every situation, trust God.

The first two, watchfulness and prayer, sometimes are mentioned together in the Bible. *Watch and pray* is therefore excellent advice for Christians. These two words are complementary, not exclusive, for if we are not watchful (observant, alert) how shall we know what to pray about? And if we don't learn details of a situation requiring prayer, how can we know what to watch for?

We have seen that, in the context of this book, Jesus spent more time talking about watchfulness than prayer. This, however, is not true of the entire Bible.

Rather, the opposite. Prayer usually takes precedence. It is involved with two of the four basic requirements for spiritual revival: Pray, and seek the Lord's face. The second is an idiom referring to intense prayer. (2 Chronicles 7:14)

Watchfulness and prayer were mentioned together by Jesus several times in the New Testament. The first time he linked the two, on the night after he delivered his end-time speech, he asked his disciples to keep watch while he prayed at Gethsemane. They fell asleep, for the first of three times, and he said to them:

"Could you men not keep watch with me for one hour? Watch and pray so that you will not fall into temptation. The spirit is willing but the body is weak." (Mat. 26:40-41)

For the disciples whom Jesus was instructing, the admonition to watch and pray had to do with personal frailty. For every human being, an important thing to watch for (anticipate) is temptation. This can come in many forms, but if we are prayerful and watchful, we will recognize it and will not fall into the lure of sin.

Jesus prayed second and third times, expressing his desire for God the Father to deliver him from the murderous scene that was about to take place. But he acknowledged willingness to see it through, if it was the Father's will.

The disciples fell asleep again…and again. After the third time, with torches partially lighting the scene, Judas identified Jesus to the Jewish leaders and they arrested him while the disciples were still half asleep.

The scene closed with this devastating comment by Matthew: "Then all the disciples deserted him and fled." (Mat. 26:56)

Failure of the disciples to watch and pray left them, and Jesus, in vulnerable positions. Jesus, who had stayed alert (watchful), and had prayed through it all, spoke calmly to the angry crowd before they led him away.

Contrast that to the disciples, who had neither watched nor prayed. They panicked. And they were not even targets of the assassins.

Here we have a lesson so clear that the underlying principles seem almost redundant: We need to obey everything Jesus says to us through his word (the Bible). Among these things are the requirements, under difficult circumstances, to be watchful (awake, alert) and prayerful.

We should talk to God about everything, but especially those things that could affect our own lives, family members, friends and neighbors. We should pray for the eternal salvation of everyone we know.

We should pray for our church, the pastor(s) and other members. We should pray about personal and professional situations and problems. If married, our prayers should be as much about our spouse, children and extended family as ourselves.

We should pray for the salvation of every unbeliever we know and be prepared to share the gospel with anyone willing to listen.

The status of our national liberties can affect all of us in many ways, so we should pray daily for our nation. Right now, these liberties are under the most insidious attack launched directly against the U.S.A. since Pearl Harbor. It may not end with a bombing. But it has been stated by U.S. enemies, foreign and domestic, that, by armed revolution if necessary, they intend to change this nation from its current freedom-based structure as a republic into a socialist dictatorship.

Prayer was never more needful than now for concerned Americans.

Important Things

The things emphasized most by Jesus in his end-time sermon were descriptive details of preliminary celestial events including the sign of his Second

Coming and descriptive details of what, to Bible students, has come to be known as *great tribulation* (Mat. 24:21). A better translation of the original Greek words than *great tribulation* is *severe persecution*.

Jesus' talk was for believers, beginning with the apostolic era. In it he said nothing to indicate that any believers, alive at the time, would elude this persecution. No matter what our theology, it would be wise to prepare ourselves for the worst and do a lot of praying about it. The apostles did neither and wound up fleeing in terror, even though none of them was the primary target.

Jesus was.

We need to pray about every aspect of persecution mentioned by Jesus. To me, the most horrible is that many Christians will betray each other and/or deny their Lord and Savior. I pray that I shall not be among those who deny Jesus or betray fellow believers. This, to me, is the most important end-time prayer.

I pray further that the Holy Spirit will keep my family members, friends and other believers from denying the Lord or betraying one another. Jesus said that individual family members would betray one another, so we can anticipate horrible treatment at the hands of Jesus-haters, many of whom already are identifiable. This will become even more of an issue as we proceed further into what the Bible calls the end-time or the time of the end.

Great tribulation is covered by No. 1 in the list below. This and all of the other mentioned themes should be committed to prayer before they happen and/or while occurring:

1. Persecution of believers for the sake of Jesus in all nations (Mat. 24:9). This is escalating. The U.S.A. is included because Congress, early in 2021, passed a bill that negates constitutional religious freedoms enjoyed by Christians. Pray for these to be restored.
2. Jesus said he would shorten the period of tribulation (persecution) for the sake of the elect (Mat. 24:22). According to prophetic scriptures, that period of time is to be about 3½ years. Pray that the "shortening" will reduce it so that it won't last more than three years.
3. Watch out for the deception of false Christs. Recognize as an imposter anyone who has his feet on the ground. When Jesus returns, it will be a celestial event: We will "meet him in the air." (cp 1 Th. 4:17; Mat. 24:4, 24:31). Pray that you and those you love will not be deceived.
4. Watch out for false prophets. These are already present and Christians are being deceived. Recognize a false prophet as one who makes a single errant prediction. The Holy Spirit, inspirer of Bible prophecy, never errs (Mat. 24:11, Rev. 22:18-19). Pray for discernment.

5. Wars, threats of war, famines and earthquakes. These are difficult to identify as end-time events because they happen so often. But it does seem as if there have been more wars, martial threats and natural disasters lately than usual (Mat. 24:5-7). Pray for deliverance.
6. Although not mentioned by Jesus in his end-time sermon, events of recent history have shown that previews of successful socialistic revolutions are gun confiscation – so citizens won't be able to protect themselves – and nationwide economic collapse. Pray for guidance.
7. Jesus described the work of the invading forces as the "abomination that causes desolation." (Mat. 24:16-22) This phrase creates a vision of events so horrible that the Lord said when believers recognize it they should take flight. Pray for recognition.

The Abomination of Desolation

Identification of the desolater is a mystery. A good No. 1 guess is China, Russia and others from the Communist world and No. 2 Iran and others in the Muslim world. These are hostile to nations such as the U.S.A. which still enjoy some freedoms. There are many socialists in high positions already in the U.S.A.

The U.S.A just completed a year in which violent demonstrators, many of them associated with radical groups such as Antifa, encouraged by Marxists, destroyed the downtown areas of major cities while murdering police officers, mostly by sniper fire. They made 24 unsuccessful attempts to assassinate then-President Trump. During these attacks, members of Trump's protective detail were injured.

Pray for an end to the violence, and for arrest and prosecution of the criminals, regardless of political affiliation, who are being encouraged to break the law. Most of the decisions to prevent law enforcers from actively trying to arrest and prosecute the violent criminals have come from mayors of large cities. Some state governors also have been involved. Pray for their removal from office, and/or launch petition drives for their recall. California's governor is being targeted for removal because of dictatorial actions.

The Lord gave instruction for his people to take flight when they recognize a destroyer in the Holy Place (Mat. 24:15-16). In the Jewish temple and tabernacle, the Holy Place was an enclosed room containing sacred objects. Equivalent to that in Christendom is the church sanctuary where worship and preaching take place.

We may view this, therefore, from a Christian perspective, as pertaining to churches and their contents. Most Jews today do not believe the New Testament, in which Jesus is quoted saying these things. He is talking here to Christians.

He gave a strange instruction to pray that the flight does not take place in winter or on the Sabbath because of the distress involved, especially for pregnant women (Mat. 24:19-21). Almost every Christian will pray if and when this happens, so Jesus is filling a gap with the prayer about winter, which might not be a usual part of such a prayer.

There was a good reason for Jesus mentioning winter flight. I know an experienced camper who says that exposure to the cold is the No. 1 killer of people attempting to live in the wild.

Fleeing from one's home at any time presents many problems. Not the least of these, as the Israelites discovered during their flight through the wilderness, is finding sufficient food and water.

This may sound strange, but I am praying for manna. The manna came down from above for the fleeing Israelites (John 6:31). I believe it may have originated on a comet that lurked nearby in an orbital pattern throughout their wanderings. If a comet produced and discharged manna once for God's people to eat, why can't it happen again?

But if there is to be no manna, the people in flight will face similar circumstances to the original Christian settlers of the United States, who were fleeing persecution by European tyrants.

It is a good idea for all of us to do a lot of reading on the subject a.s.a.p. and acquire the things suggested by experienced outdoorsmen. It's also a good idea to find in advance the sparsely populated area to which we decide to flee, if and when necessary. The ideal place would have plenty of wildly growing edible plants and a large body of water nearby, well stocked with fish.

End-time flight could be associated with invasion, as was the flight from Jerusalem perpetrated by the Roman invasion in 66-70 a. d. Jesus did not instruct his followers to do battle with the invaders, so it does not seem that he wants us to engage in any sort of violence, even on the defensive. He is consistent about this, because in a similar situation he took a sword out of Peter's hands.

The Roman invasion of Jerusalem is believed by many Bible interpreters, including myself, to have been a preview of events preceding Jesus' Second Coming. At that time, a comet appeared in the sky.

Another similarity between the siege and destruction of Jerusalem in 66-70 a. d. and the great tribulation of the end-time is the time element. The Jerusalem event lasted about 3½ years. Jesus predicted that the end-time event would have similar duration. According to the book of Revelation's end-time prophecy, the duration of great tribulation will be 1260 days (Rev. 12:6) or 42 months (Rev. 13:5).

These are not contradictory prophecies. Both are equivalent to about 3½ years. However, Jesus did state that for the sake of believers who suffer during the great tribulation, he would shorten that time period (Mat. 24:22).

There is a possibility that we are misinterpreting what Jesus meant when he said he would shorten the tribulation time period. He may not have meant that he would reduce it to less than 3½ years. The fact that this time period is stated second and third times to be of this same duration (42 months, 1260 days) may incline the meaning to a second interpretation.

This would be that Jesus will shorten that time to be "only" 3½ years when, in fact, without his intervention, it would be much longer. But here's the main point. However long the period of tribulation is, it is likely to be similar to the scary period of time just before Jesus' return. There are many biblical descriptions of this post-tribulation time period. One of the best is Isaiah 2:9-22.

We know from what Jesus prophesied that the period of great tribulation will be created by human terrorists, perhaps Communists and/or Muslims. After God shortens that, as He has promised, and revives and restores His people, the terror will begin for the terrorists.

Because God is just, it seems probable that the terrorists will be terrified by events originating in celestial (heavenly) spheres also for about three or 3½ years. Thus, the terrorists will undergo terrorism for the same length of time as the people they terrorized. Frightened people often turn to the Lord, and so will many of the terrorists.

God is just. This is the kind of perfect justice that characterizes Him. But He doesn't stop with justice. To that He adds love. It is His will that all people be saved and come to the knowledge of the truth. And so this time period – however long – will present opportunity for the entire remnant of human beings to accept the eternal salvation He offers to the sincerely repentant who decide to trust Him.

Forgiveness and Repentance

What does He want of us with respect to violent enemies? His instruction is to love them as He does. We have just been reminded that it is His will that all be saved (spiritually) and brought to the knowledge of truth that leads to a heavenly destination (1 Tim. 2:4).

But this must begin for everyone (relatives, friends and enemies) with sincere confession and repentance of sins. In the case of those who have destroyed houses of God and murdered or attempted to murder worshippers, the act of repentance could be problematic. Forgiveness immediately follows confession of sin, but full repentance (change of lifestyle) requires deeper commitment.

The bottom line is that Jesus wants us to keep in direct communication with him at all times, no matter what is happening. It becomes more urgent to pray when our lives and churches are threatened. But doesn't it make sense that one who talks to Jesus all the time about everything may be more fluent in crisis prayer than one who is out of touch?

Luke summarized two of our first three chapter themes in the final verse he wrote concerning Jesus' end-time speech: "Be always on the watch, and pray that you may be able to escape all that is about to happen, and that you may be able to stand before the Son of Man." (Luke 21:36)

Let's end this chapter with instructive words by Jesus about prayer and fasting: "When you pray, do not be like the hypocrites, for they love to pray standing in the synagogues and on the street corners to be seen by men. I tell you the truth. They have received their reward in full.

"When you pray, go into your room, close the door and pray to your Father, who is unseen. Then your Father, who sees what is done in secret, will reward you.

"And when you pray, do not keep on babbling like pagans, for they think they will be heard because of their many words. Do not be like them, for your Father knows what you need before you ask him.

"This is how you should pray:

"'Our Father in heaven, hallowed be your name. Your kingdom come, your will be done on earth as it is in heaven. Give us today our daily bread. Forgive us our sins as we have forgiven those who sin against us. And lead us not into temptation, but deliver us from the evil one, for yours is the kingdom and the power and the glory forever. Amen.'

"If you forgive men when they sin against you, your heavenly Father will also forgive you. But if you do not forgive men their sins, your Father will not forgive your sins.

"When you fast, do not look somber as the hypocrites do, for they disfigure their faces to show men they are fasting. I tell you the truth: they have received their reward in full. But when you fast, put oil on your head and wash your face, so that it will not be obvious to men that you are fasting, but only to your Father, who is unseen, and your Father, who sees what is done in secret, will reward you." (Mat. 6:5-18)

If we watch and pray, as the Bible defines these things, our lives should attain the spiritual stature God intends for us.

CHAPTER FOUR

PREPARE AND SHARE

In his end-time sermon, the two rhyming words in this chapter's title were emphasized by Jesus. The Lord wants us to make advance preparation so that we are ready at all times to share Scriptural reasons for our faith in Jesus Christ.

This theme will be focalized during the final days of the end-time when millions, perhaps hundreds of millions, are saved by being brought to the knowledge of the truth. (1 Tim. 2:4)

Bottom line is this: Jesus suffered persecution, bled and died, in the place of all who trust in him, so our eternal destination can be changed from hell to heaven: "God made him who had no sin to be sin for us, so that in him we might become the righteousness of God." (2 Cor. 5:21).

Millions will turn from paganism to Christ during the closing days of this planet's existence. At that time, if we have been trusting in the Lord, we shall be ready, on the last day, to rise and spend forever with Him on the new "earth." (Rev. 21:1)

Jesus said in his sermon: "So you also must be ready, because the Son of Man will come at an hour when you do not expect him." (Mat. 24:44)

Peter wrote concerning personal preparation: "In your hearts set apart Christ as Lord. Always be prepared to give an answer to everyone who asks you to give the reason for the hope that you have. But do this with gentleness and respect." (1 Peter 3:15).

In other words, don't try to jam the Gospel down the throats of unbelievers. Some evangelists are intimidators. They exaggerate when they estimate the number of people they have brought to the Lord. Actually, it's doubtful if they have brought any.

Responses to aggressive messages that may be interpreted as salvation experiences, likely are efforts to seem agreeable so that, as quickly as possible, the targets of intimidation can flee the scene. Their so-called professions of faith may not be real.

Survival and Revival

Let's discuss spiritual reawakening, otherwise known as revival, and basic survival. There are many scriptures indicating that a great revival will take place at the end of the age and multitudes of people, many of them terrified by celestial and terrestrial events, will be saved. That is to say, they will be brought to the knowledge of the truth about the meaning for them personally of the sacrificial death and glorious resurrection of Jesus Christ.

My favorite Bible verse expressing this theme, which clearly is about the end-time because it mentions the day of the Lord (when Jesus returns), is Joel 3:14: "Multitudes, multitudes (read that 'millions upon millions') in the valley of decision! For the day of the Lord is near in the valley of decision."

The scary scenario will involve earth crumbling under what perhaps will be a fusillade from a deadly comet. It will be the occasion for frightened human beings to have one more chance to decide to place their eternal destination in the trustworthy care of the Lord and Savior, Jesus Christ.

Were the prophesied end of the human habitation of this planet not so frightening, would so many be saved? We should not even wonder about this because God has foreseen and planned the final scene of life on earth. It is his desire for all to be saved and come to the knowledge of the truth (1 Tim. 2:4).

He never has, nor ever will He force anyone to turn their lives over to Him. But the argument for trusting Jesus has never been as persuasive as it will be at the very end of time.

Those who have fled from danger at the behest of Jesus (Mat. 24:16-21) will come to understand that, wherever that flight has taken them, the refuge has been only temporary.

No matter where they find themselves, whether in crumbling mountain caves about to crash down upon their heads, or near seas where tidal waves threaten, the choice between eternal life in either heaven or hell will be clarified.

And the response time will be reduced to meet deadline pressures.

During my lifetime I have known three men who became Christians because something frightened them.

One was a soldier, Archie Parrish, who didn't think he would survive a terrifying battlefield with his life. He did survive, and the first free time he had after that, he sought out a Christian pastor and asked him what he had to do to be saved. The pastor explained to him that he needed to believe that when Jesus died on the cross, He took upon himself the sins of everyone who believes and commits his or her life to Him as personal savior. Jesus then rose from the dead to confirm the accomplishment. (Romans 1:4)

Parrish later was ordained to the ministry and became the international director of Evangelism Explosion. EE Director D. James Kennedy put him in charge of training my wife Joan and I for a 20-week session of EE. By that time he was a committed Christian whose ability to share the Gospel was remarkable.

He was something like the jailer in the biblical book of Acts, who asked the same question when he feared for his life at the hands of Roman soldiers. He believed prisoners had escaped during an earthquake that damaged the jail under his watch. He thought he would receive the death penalty.

There had been no actual escape, but Paul, who was in the jail at the time, told him how he could be "saved" from eternal hellfire instead of physical death, which was not really imminent as he believed. The jailer and the rest of his family committed themselves to Jesus and found out that, since there had been no escape, his life would be spared.

The second man was a co-worker, John Maddrey. One day at the office he told me he noticed that I was different from others who worked there because I did not curse: I did not use the name of Jesus in the process of uttering an oath.

He told me that since he had found out he had terminal cancer he knew he needed to do some things to set his life in order. One of them, he said, was to become a believer headed for heaven instead of a sinner bound for hell. He told me he wanted to become a Christian. I told him how and he prayed. He confessed his sins and asked Jesus to forgive him. A few months later he died.

The third case involved a man, Ed Jordan, who thought that he was on his way to hell because of terrible things he had done. Perhaps this came from the Holy Spirit, because this man, who had not been ordained or even born-again at that time, turned his life over to the Lord and soon thereafter felt the leading of the Holy Spirit to become a pastor. At the time I knew him, he was an assistant pastor at a church in Fort Lauderdale. He later became pastor of a prominent church in the state of Maryland.

Physical Evidence & Fishing Gear

My book, *The High Sign*, discusses in detail more than 200 points of physical evidence that a huge comet, with a tail millions of miles long, in appearance from earth as being stripped across the sky from horizon to horizon, will be the sign of Jesus' Second Coming. (Mat. 24:27) A shorter but still persuasive treatment of the same subject appears in my book, *Day of the Lord*.

In the final chapter of *End-Time Living*, we shall discuss basic information geared toward survival of the tribulation period. However, it is recommended that everyone reading this book do personal research by also reading books written by survivalists.

Reading alone is not enough. Since it is evident that we have entered the era described in the Bible as the end-time, reading survivalist books is just the first step. Even now we should begin familiarizing ourselves with equipment we shall need (in my case fishing gear).

We need to get started on this because no one knows how much time we have until the outset of worldwide tribulation prophesied by Jesus. A lot of people will die of unnatural causes. Jesus said if that time were not shortened, no one would be left alive on earth. (Mat. 24:22)

I, for one, would like to stay alive during the exciting final time period, when millions of frightened souls will hear the Gospel and begin trusting Jesus for eternal salvation.

Some of them may hear the good news from you or me.

CHAPTER FIVE

FIRM AND FEARLESS

Of the three Gospel writers who quoted from Jesus' end-time sermon, only Luke cited parts of the speech dealing with the theme of fear. This probably reflected the fact that, of the three, the physician Luke probably encountered more human fears in his medical practice than the other two in their professional lives. Matthew was a tax collector. We don't know what Mark's profession was.

Jesus often told his followers not to be afraid of their circumstances, so we can presume from this that he considered fearlessness to be an important character trait for his disciples. The following are paraphrases from his sermon:

- Do not fear war; don't even worry about it. (Luke 21:9)
- If threatened by persecution, don't worry. (Luke 21:14)
- Do not be afraid of fleeing a besieged city. (Luke 21:22)

- Don't be terrified if earth and sky are shaken. (Luke 21:26)

The preceding events were predicted by Jesus to take place before His return (Luke 21:27). He wants us to look forward happily to this event because when it is about to happen, he said we should stand and lift up our heads in anticipation (Luke 21:28). At this time, all fear should disappear…and then will follow the ascension into heaven of resurrected dead and living believers. Far from being terrified, we should await these things with joyful expectation.

Jesus' final word on this topic appeared in Luke 21:36: "Be always on the watch, and pray that you may be able to escape all that is about to happen, and that you may be able to stand before the Son of Man."

Isn't it interesting how the basic principles tie together during the most significant events? Here, for the second time within a single context, we encounter the word *stand*.

This word, when used by Jesus, referred to much more than a physical posture. Often, in these texts, the adverb *firm* appears with the verb *stand*. Jesus told his disciples to stand firm when they faced frightening and/or challenging circumstances.

Unlike some faiths, Christianity is not an idolatrous religion of fear. It is first of faith, second of trust. In every situation, Jesus wants us to believe He can handle it and that we can trust Him to do whatever is right. There are rare occasions when He does something that we may not believe is fair or just. But always we must trust Him because He is God and does not make mistakes.

A Firm Stance

The picture of someone with a firm stance is clearly portrayed in baseball by the batter leaning in anticipation toward the pitcher who is about to throw a pitch. This appropriately is called a batting stance.

In the vernacular of Jesus, however, standing firm meant something different. Both words were important. For a Christian the concept of standing firm means determination not to waver from a position of righteousness even under duress. It is an expansion of the concept we have already mentioned, that of great tribulation (persecution).

If the persecution becomes physical – and in the case of religious persecution it usually does – the persecuted one may remain standing spiritually even when his/her body is taking such a beating that physically staying on the feet becomes impossible. This kind of brutality seems to become commonplace whenever and wherever Communist atheism and/or Islamic terrorism become dominant.

A suggestion: After finishing this book, read one by Richard Wurmbrand. Do so, and you will have no need for explanation of any kind about what it means, as far as God is concerned, for his people to stand firm. It means staying faithful and affirming (not denying) Him no matter how bad things seem to be. This may not be possible for most people undergoing physical persecution. But it is for a Christian trusting wholeheartedly in Jesus.

In Jesus' sermon he said that, under this kind of affliction, most people would yield. He said believers should not fear or even worry about what is taking place: "This will result in your being witnesses to (unbelievers). But make up your mind not to worry beforehand how you will defend yourselves. For I will give you words and wisdom that none of your adversaries will be able to resist or contradict." (Luke 21:13)

He said persecution will become so intense in all nations that family members will betray one another: "You will be betrayed even by parents, brothers, relatives and friends, and they will put some of you to death. All men will hate you because of me. But not a hair of your head will perish." (Luke 21:16-18).

The last sentence of the paragraph above refers to eternal life in heaven with God, not the life expectancy on earth which may come to a sudden end.

Standing firm here means betraying no one and refusing to deny faith in Jesus Christ. The attempt to coerce believers into denying their faith is one of the primary goals of demon-energized men. Satan already has plenty of human subjects, but he wants more to spend eternity in hell with him. Coercion is used by his minions as they try to intimidate us to deny our Lord.

The physical pain may be severe, but if we talk to the Lord all the way through it and determine that our love for Him is stronger than any physical harm that may come to us, we shall be faithful to Him in standing firm.

Do not under any circumstances give in to the oppressors. Don't agree with anything they say or fear anything they threaten to do. "By standing firm you will gain life." (Luke 21:19)

Standing firm during persecution is such an important end-time topic that, in this case, repetition is emphatic. Matthew added a few things to what Luke had to say from the text of Jesus' sermon. My favorite is the embellishing of the admonition to *stand firm* so that it included the words *to the end*.

Speaking primarily of eternal, not temporal salvation, Matthew quoted Jesus: "He who stands firm to the end will be saved." (Mt. 24:13)

Mark's repetition enhances the emphasis: "All men will hate you because of me, but he who stands firm to the end will be saved." (Mark 13:13)

To this statement Jesus added something that seems supplementary to the stand-firm concept. He said, "And this gospel of the kingdom will be preached in the whole world as a testimony to all nations, and then the end will come." (Mat. 24:14)

Preaching of the gospel to multitudes and seeing so many saved that the worldwide number of people headed for heaven rises to one out of every three will be the ultimate outcome. Zechariah described this plainly in the concluding section of his prophetic book about the end-tine:

"In the whole earth," declares the Lord, "Two-thirds will be struck down and perish, yet one-third will be left in it. This third I will bring into the fire; I will refine them like silver and test them like gold. They will call on my name and I will answer them; I will say, 'They are my people,' and they will say, 'The Lord is our God.'" (Zech. 13:8-9, 14:9)

Assuming that this is being read mostly by citizens of the United States of America, we live in the nation that for more than 200 years has maintained the highest percentage of Christians per capita in the world. It is possible that at one time this number was 50% or more.

Today, with most of the so-called millennial generation as yet to believe in Christ, the number is about 25%. Still about 50% of the total U.S.A. population call themselves Christians, but at least half of these are not yet actually born-again and headed for heaven. Neither are the pastors of more than half of their churches. Billy Graham and D. James Kennedy made these estimations of the numbers based on lifetimes of experience in evangelism.

Some nations have not been effectively reached as yet by evangelistic teams. Based on statistics I have seen attributed to Graham and have heard Kennedy say, it seems unlikely that as many as 10% of the world population is Christian at this time. The number 5% may be closer to the truth.

It is difficult to contemplate the vast numbers to be saved during the final few years of this world's existence in order to bring this number up to one-third.

CHAPTER SIX

MORAL DISSIPATION

In the English language the word *immorality* often refers to improper sexual activity. An immoral person fails to uphold traditional standards by having premarital sex and/or cheating on his/her spouse. However, the words *moral* and *immoral* have broader meaning than that. They refer to generally accepted principles of right and wrong.

A Bible-reading believer has no difficulty ascertaining whether an activity is sinful or not. The greatest of all books makes clear distinctions.

Oswald Chambers used only eight words in his famous moral instruction for believers that is here being quoted for the second time in this book: *Give up the right to yourself to Him.* By Him, Chambers could have meant either God the Father, God the Son, God the Holy Spirit, or the Trinitarian three-in-one. He probably meant Jesus, God's Son, because it was He who shed his blood and died to make our sins forgivable. He is known as the Word of God (John 1:1).

If He made clear anywhere in His book that He was displeased with human beings when they misbehaved, we are safe in saying that as far as He is concerned, that form of misbehavior is immoral, i.e., sinful.

We shouldn't do it.

When we do it, we should confess it to God as sin.

When we confess, He forgives. *If we confess our sins, he is faithful and just and will forgive us our sins and purify us from all unrighteousness. (1 John 1:9)*

After that we are spiritually clean, until we commit another sin. Speaking for myself, I'm sure I have committed sins of which I have been unaware. I don't know how God handles that because these sins were not confessed.

If I feel an inner conviction that I have sinned in a certain matter and don't confess, well, I don't even like to think about that. I have no clue what God does about it, but perhaps that is part of a judgmental process that everyone, even Christians, undergo at the outset of the afterlife. (Rom. 14:10, 2 Cor. 5:10)

At that time, we do know for sure, however, that if we have committed ourselves to Jesus Christ as Lord and Savior and have tried to make full confession of known sins to Him, we shall take up residence forever in heaven with Him.

The Self Life

This is a good place for more consideration of the Chambers quote about giving up personal rights to God. There is in the dictionary I use a list of about 500 compound words in the English language containing the word *self*. My choice for the basic word is *self-centeredness*. I think most of the others could be categorized as derivatives from this catalyst for all kinds of sins.

Many of the *self* words refer to bad attitude or misbehavior. This is sin. Even a word like self-reliance, which seems on the surface to be a good thing, really isn't. It is self-reliance that so often gets us into trouble.

What I need to do when I am in a difficult situation is to commit everything I am doing to God. This may be called *God-reliance*, and it's an excellent way to avoid sinning against Him. It's immeasurably superior to self-reliance.

The following are "self" words describing bad attitudes and behavior: self-adulatory, self-anointed, self-approbation, self-complacency, self-contempt, self-debasement, self-deception, self-deification, self-deluded, self-denigration, self-deprecation, self-engrossed, self-exhibiting, self-guided, self-hating, self-idolatry, self-inflated, self-loathing, self-mockery, self-obsessed, self-ordained, self-oriented, self-pleasing, self-praise, self-preoccupied, self-promoting, self-righteousness, self-validation, self-worship.

A shorter list of behavior to practice comes from chapter ten of the Exodus describing the Ten Commandments. Here is a compacted version:

- Worship no one other than the Bible's God.
- Do not make or buy anything to be worshiped.
- Do not use the name of Jesus in a curse.
- Worship and honor God one day each week.
- Treat your father and mother respectfully.
- Do not murder.
- Limit your sexual activity to your spouse.
- Do not steal.
- Do not tell lies about anyone or anything.
- Do not covet things that are not yours.

Sin won't be different during the end-time from any other time. If God gives instructions not to do something, as Jesus did numerous times in his two great sermons, we shouldn't do it. If he categorizes something as displeasing to Himself without explicitly calling it sin or giving instructions to avoid it, we still shouldn't do it. Here is an illustration:

Then Jesus said to His disciples, "If anyone wants to walk after me, he must deny himself, take up his cross and follow me. For whoever wants to save his life shall lose it, but whoever loses his life for me shall find it." (Mat. 16:24-25) This is a perfect starting place for us, with *self*-denial. It is one of very few good things associated with self, because it is the opposite of self-centeredness.

Besides personal sin, another related problem for a Christian is to give positive reinforcement to another believer's sin. This is actually a double sin, for both the one sinning and the one encouraging the sinner.

Here's an example from Jesus, referring not to obvious sin, but to the teaching of false doctrine. This comes from His end-time sermon: "Watch out that no one deceives you. For many will come in my name, claiming, 'I am the Christ,' and will deceive many." (Mat. 24:4-5)

There have been teachers of false doctrine within the community of Christians ever since the first century a. d. In some cases, it is based on ignorance, but even so it is inexcusable and may be defined as sin, because it involves rejecting truth.

If a teacher isn't sure he has determined truth, he should not yet teach on that subject. All he should do is ask questions and see if someone under his authority has a valid response.

Most false doctrines are based not upon ignorance, but selfish motives. Often, the motive is self-enrichment. For instance, Christians have made a lot of money by writing books containing provably incorrect doctrines. Some of these doctrines, especially one having to do with what has come to be known as the rapture (ascension) of believers, are now contentious.

For instance, the aspect of rapture now commonly described as "pre-trib" (before tribulation) is so controversial that there is at present about an even split among people claiming to be Christian as to its validity. A lot of money has changed hands based on books and radio and TV interviews for pre-trib rapture spokesmen, pro and con. Anyone who has taken and/or promoted a posture on this issue primarily in anticipation of lucrative benefits, regardless of the verity of his position, has committed a sin.

One who is simply speaking out of ignorance probably is not innocent of wrongdoing, either. But he/she who claims knowledge of fact that he/she does not actually have is either lying (a sin) or self-deceived. I wouldn't want the Lord to catch me doing this because it certainly isn't harmless to those who believe it after hearing it taught by a respected Bible teacher. Instead of teaching something like this, I'd probably ask my class: "What do you think? Is this a sin or not?"

If you want to encounter false teaching, all you have to do is watch Christian TV. Yes, Christian TV is better than "fake news" and other worldly alternatives, but as Christians are we to believe that our leaders should be teaching things that are not scriptural, when there is no excuse for it? There are enough Bibles available in the U.S.A. for every believer who can read to possess at least one. Some organizations give them away.

So, really, for teaching false doctrine, whether the motive is based on ignorant misunderstanding or personal benefit, there is no excuse.

Because of the rapid advancement of evil, it appears that we may be approaching the dangerous period of the end-time known as *great tribulation*. The persecution is so great in some nations that they appear to be there already. If we are indeed at the outset of the end-time, as it does appear we are, here is a list of things we should be doing from now until Jesus comes back:

- Taking care to avoid being deceived. (Mat. 24:4)
- Refusing to acknowledge false Christs. (Mat. 24:5, 24-26)
- Loving those who hate us, even persecutors. (Mat. 24:9, 12)
- Resisting efforts to force us to deny Christ. (Mat. 24:10)
- Rejecting efforts to make us betray one another. (Mat. 24:10)
- Refuting prophets who speak in error. (Mat. 24:11, 24)
- Standing firm in resistance to demonic spirits. (Mat. 24:13)
- Watching, preparing for the Lord's return. (Mat. 24:42-44)
- Praying about all of these things.

CHAPTER SEVEN

TRUSTING A TRUSTWORTHY GOD

There is not a specific command in either of Jesus' mountainside sermons to trust God in every situation. But it is a principle that is covered broadly by numerous scriptures including this one: "Trust in the Lord with all your heart and do not rely on your own understanding. In all your ways, acknowledge Him and He will direct your paths." (Prov. 3:5)

Lord, even as I write this, I acknowledge you. I am in a terrible situation that seems to get worse and worse. Help!

This situation has been worsening for the past two years. It began with an apparently small error on my income tax return, prepared during the winter of 2019 for the year 2018. My wife Joan had died in March of 2018, but the professional doing the return for me that year named myself, and not Joan, as no-longer living. In checking over the return, I overlooked that mistake and so it was submitted to IRS with the error.

Several phone calls to IRS later, we thought the issue had been corrected when I received a tax refund for the year 2018.

How wrong we were!

Instead of corrected, the issue was compounded. In summer of 2020, with IRS understaffed and many of its offices closed due to CCP Virus precautions, it became difficult to reach IRS by phone (The lines were backed up for hours.).

In September of 2020, instead of receiving my 2019 refund as expected, I got a letter from IRS stating that they would not issue a refund or even process my return. They said according to their records I was dead. They did state correctly that Joan was deceased but had failed to correct the error of my demise.

Think about how ridiculous this was. If I were dead, as they now have me described in their computer, how could I have had a return prepared and sent to them at all? Why would a professional, obviously knowing her client was dead, prepare that return? Where would I have gotten all those income-related documents for the year 2019 that were included with the return? And, why were they writing a letter to a dead guy?

Anyway, at that time the IRS said they could not process the return or issue a refund. They mentioned two issues they wanted clarified. One concerned ID theft. The other was social security.

Neither was a valid issue.

One year later, my return for 2020 has been filed, but I still have not received the 2019 refund or stimulus payments I have qualified for.

Enough for details. The biggest problem has been my reaction. I have been a nervous wreck, at times, difficult to get along with. I have not been living according to the divine principles of the Bible, especially this most important one: Trusting God.

Jesus said that Christians should worry about nothing, but be prayerful to God about everything (Php. 4:6). We are to trust God in every situation.

I have not been doing that.

I suspect that the primary reason why the situation has been getting worse and worse is my failure to trust God.

Even now that I understand what I have been doing wrong, I am still subject to worry. I lay awake in bed for three hours fretting about the situation on the night before writing this.

I am not the only Christian in the world who disobeys God through worry. In fact, I have never heard one deny that he/she was susceptible to anxiety.

When will we learn?

Our present situations, however worrisome, are nothing compared with what we can expect during end-time tribulation. That will become so bad, according to Jesus, that at one point we will have to flee from our homes.

Personally speaking, if I can't cope with an IRS problem, how will I deal with full-blast persecution?

This issue faces every Christian alive today, for we seem to be at the outset of the time of the end. These believers include the author and readers of this book.

Ultimately, each of us should go beyond trivial things such as an IRS problem and ask ourselves if we can stand firm, as Jesus commands, during what threatens to be the worst period of persecution in world history. (Mat. 24:21-22).

If we are unsure that we can stand firm, it means we need to pray and pray some more that God will see us through to the end. And we must trust completely that He will do so.

Dead or Alive?

The way things are now, IRS considers both my wife and I dead. At least, they are half right. And, I suppose, the only sensible explanation for receiving a tax return from deceased individuals is that it must be ID fraud.

What it actually is, is IRS employees failing to put accurate records into their computer. This occurred before they refunded my 2018 return. But now, they are refusing to consider my returns because of an error that we thought was corrected two years ago.

I know it doesn't make sense.

But, lately, I have come to realize that it's not an issue for IRS. I don't even know those people, and it's certainly understandable how, with offices closed or understaffed, and just about everything being done over the phone, at the end of the day the workers don't have the energy left to do a lot of computer work.

Blame it on dictatorial politics concerning the CCP (Chinese Communist Party) virus, if you will.

But even as I write this, I have a picture in my mind of God sadly shaking His head. He is saying: "You just don't get it!"

It has been only a short time since I figured out this much: God is not pleased that I have allowed anxiety to plummet to new depths for me. He knows that I have memorized the simple Bible verse: *Be anxious about nothing!*

I don't know about you, but this verse right now is for me.

Think about it, Christian friends. I know the year 2020 was a tough one for almost all Americans other than a few elitists. But that is no excuse for us to stop trusting God.

2020 was a picnic compared with the *great tribulation* (correct translation: *intense persecution*) prophesied by Jesus for the end-time. I don't know about you, but if I can't trust Him through a minor problem such as an IRS error that might cost me a few thousand dollars, it is very doubtful if I can stand firm through persecution as Jesus described it:

"Then you will be handed over and put to death, and you will be hated in all nations because of me. At that time, many will turn away from the faith and will betray and hate each other, and many false prophets will appear and deceive many people." (Mat. 24:9-11)

The point of this is not to hate the IRS. It's more personal than that.

The Bible says: "Trust in the Lord with all your heart. Do not rely on your own understanding. In all your ways acknowledge him and he will direct your paths." (Prov. 3:5).

If I were trusting God, according to scriptural guidelines, resting in full confidence upon the One who, according to the same scriptures, loves me and never makes mistakes, I would not have wasted one minute during the past year and a half on worry.

It is nowhere near as bad as it is going to get for all of us, according to these words of Jesus in his great end-time sermon: "Then there will be great tribulation, unequaled from the beginning of the world until now." (Mat. 24:21)

The worst ever? How will a chronic worrier deal with that?

My worry is a sign of failure to trust God. I think He considers this a sin. I know I do. How could I not trust the God who has been faithful to me for so many years in so many ways?

Trusting God may not be an issue at all for an atheist, but it's a big one for a Christian.

I have been a believer in the God of the Bible for as long as I have memory. I was probably in first or second grade when I began to believe. And yet, there have been times between then and now when I have worried myself into fits of near despair.

Yes, I know the Bible says, "Do not be anxious about anything...Cast all your anxiety on him because he cares for you." (Php. 4:6...1 Pet. 5:7)

These statements should be sufficient to stave off worry for everyone who believes in God. But, even though the words *believe* and *trust* sometimes are used as synonyms, in my Christian experience they have been oceans apart.

When it comes to eternal salvation, I have absolute belief that the blood Jesus shed on Calvary washed away the sins of billions of believing human beings including myself. But my trust in him to handle more mundane difficulties has been considerably less reliable.

An Amazing Story

I do trust Him...most of the time. But there have been other exceptions and the one I am about to relate had an amazing finish. It has been published, at least in part, in two other books, one of which was a collection of great true stories.

It happened during the late 1970s in Fort Lauderdale when the economy turned bad. This was shortly after Joan quit her job as head nurse on a hospital floor in order to stay home with our elementary school-aged sons, Mike and Dan.

Joan quit that job in faith that God would provide through me the finances needed by the family, even though it meant an immediate drop in income for us of about 50 percent. We discussed it with our faith-filled pastor, and he said to her:

"Go ahead and quit."

And she did.

And I worried…and worried.

Yes, I prayed: More than usual. But I don't think they can be called prayers of faith. More like prayers of desperation. I was frightened and became more scared as the days passed with no help in sight.

The bank holding our mortgage declined my request for a loan. Shortly thereafter, the dreaded message came in the mail. We had until the next Monday to come up with enough money for at least one month's mortgage payment.

It was Wednesday.

By Sunday I was a nervous wreck, but we went to church as usual. On this day I had a decision to make: Should I place my tithe check in the collection plate or should I hold onto that money until the next day? Actually, it was not a momentous decision because even with that money we were far short of having enough for the mortgage payment.

I decided to place the check in the church collection plate.

It was the first faith-based decision I had made in a while.

And then I went right back to worrying. Later in the day, when we returned to church for the evening service I had begun a countdown to the mortgage payment deadline meeting at the bank the next day.

After the service, as we were leaving, the associate pastor, Ed Jordan, whom we had not told of our problem, handed me an envelope.

He said: "The Lord told me to give this to you." And then he walked away.

In the envelope I found a check for the exact sum we needed for a single mortgage payment.

We paid that one the next day, and did not miss another until our home was paid off. The bank went out of business long before that, but our family income increased thanks to supplemental income from book sales, magazine articles and sports officiating jobs.

Within fifteen years after the crisis, we had made our final home mortgage payment and had begun paying cash for mortgage-free automobiles. We made our last mortgage payment of any kind about thirty years ago.

Is God trustworthy or what?

Here's the Bible's definitive statement from Jesus: "Come to me, all who labor and are heavy laden, and I will give you rest." (Mat. 11:28)

CHAPTER EIGHT

THE SONG OF SONGS

During most of the New Testament era *The Song of Songs*, written by a youthful King Solomon, was considered by biblical scholars to be an allegory. It was not, however, to be equated to Bunyan's *Pilgrim's Progress*.

It was superior.

Pilgrim's Progress is a fictional tale about the progress of individuals in quest of a heavenly destination, obstacles they encounter and the outcome for each. The names of Bunyan's characters tell you just about all you need to know about them. Their personalities may be inferred from their names.

This is a biblical principle. Many of the people featured in the Bible's true stories have names befitting their personalities and character traits. *The Song of Songs* accomplishes this purpose and much more despite the fact that the only named participant in the story is Solomon. The woman he is in love with is known only for the fact that she is a Shulammite. Her name is not mentioned.

She may be the Abishag mentioned in the book of 1 Kings as a servant to King David when he was near death. Abishag is there identified as a Shunammite.

Shunammite or Shulammite? The words are so similar that they could refer to the same group of people. Names of people and places may be slightly altered over the passing of years, if the descendants of the original are not great at spelling. It would be easy for the designation Shunammite (David's version) to become Shulammite (Solomon's).

Or the explanation could be as simple as a relative being hard of hearing. No, it does not prove that the Bible erred, only that either David or Solomon did.

If what is said about Abishag's caretaking of King David is true, she was selected for the job because of her extraordinary beauty, the most beautiful woman who could be found for the role of tending to the needs of the aging king.

Solomon took a good look at his father's caregiver and liked what he saw. He was so impressed that he had Adonijah put to death for requesting her hand in marriage. *The Song of Songs* seems to be a true story of the romance between Solomon and Abishag.

But it is also, almost certainly, an allegory. If it is an allegory, which, in context with the nearly three millennia that have passed since the book's writing, was the prevalent opinion of Bible scholars until very recently, it's not the only one in the Bible.

The Bible identifies the story of the Israelites' exodus from Egypt as an allegory. (1 Cor. 10:1-13)

The beginning of the story about the coming out of a hostile atmosphere in Egypt, for the allegorical interpretation, represents Christian salvation. The trek through the dry bed of the Red Sea represents water baptism. The cloud immersion, according to what Bible scholar Derek Prince concluded about thirty years ago, is Holy Spirit baptism. (Mat. 3:11, Mark 1:8, Luke 3:16)

At one time I thought the Holy Spirit baptism, in the allegory, was represented by water pouring from the rock, representing Jesus Christ.

I have come around to Prince's viewpoint.

Departure from Egypt

Scripture describes the journey on foot that followed the departure from Egypt. The Bible gives this detail about one aspect of that journey: "They all ate the same spiritual food (manna) and drank the same spiritual drink, for they drank from the spiritual rock that accompanied them, and that rock was Christ." (1 Cor. 10:3-4).

The Exodus story may indeed be studied as an allegory. In my personal studies, I have found 40 allegorical *tupos* (Greek word for *types*) in that story, which may be considered snapshots within the frame of a much larger picture.

In the Bible, Jesus is named the rock of our salvation and the cornerstone of our faith. So this figurative reference to a rock is more than just a clue that the story of the Exodus might have symbolic meaning. In combination with the rest of the figurative language about the event, it seems clearly to be an allegory.

The Greek word *tupo* is used twice in 1 Cor. 10. This tells us that the subject matter, the Exodus, is typologically figurative, i.e., allegorical. If it involved just one figurative item, that would be a different matter. But there are many.

An allegory, by definition, is a series of associated literary types.

Solomon's *Song of Songs* is a much shorter, less complicated allegory than the novel-length of the Exodus, which includes the biblical books of Exodus and Numbers. Some interpreters have included the book of Joshua in that allegory. The name Joshua is an Old Testament Hebrew rendering of the New Testament Greek name Jesus. The two names are identical.

The Song of Songs appears to be a true story of the love between Solomon and his bride, a Shulammite woman. But from a larger perspective, it represents the love shared by the divine King of kings, Jesus, and his church, which is referred to in the Bible as the bride of Christ. (Rev. 21:9)

The main characters in the Song of Songs are the bride and her loving husband. Wurmbrand, in his book *The Sweetest Song*, wrote: "The beloved can't be anybody else but Jesus."[3]

The description of the lover as a shepherd fits Jesus, who is identified figuratively in the Bible as the good shepherd. (Psalm 23) Actually, Jesus' participation in the story is as the lover, not the beloved. The beloved is the bride, that is, the church. Wurmbrand's big picture, however, is correct. This is an allegory of the love between Jesus and His church.

In this interpretation, there are various opinions as to the identity of the so-called *friends* of the bride (NIV), also known as court-ladies (KJV) and/or daughters of Jerusalem (NKJV).

The word *bride*, as it refers to the bride of Christ, includes millions of living Christians. Since the "friends" at the outset of this story seem to be spectators and not members of the bridal party (the church), they may be non-Christians or lukewarm believers. (Rev. 3:16)

These stand aside from the main plot of the story, at first, as should those who are not yet written into the "book of life" through faith in Jesus Christ. They are not yet passionate believers, but are watching the bride with interest. That interest intensifies when the bride reacts with love after being beaten by watchmen. It matures at the end with open concern for a younger sister's spiritual status.

---

[3] Richard Wurmbrand, *The Sweetest Song*, Living Sacrifice Book Co., 1988, p. 20.

There is evidence that by the end of the story these women have become true friends of the Shulammite and believers in her God. They have changed because of the faithfulness they have observed in her despite great suffering.

Let us now consider this fascinating allegory in more detail:

Song One: Sensory Love

The sensory nature of the love story between Solomon and the Shulammite is emphasized in the first seven verses of the story's first chapter. This brief text introduces all five human senses.

The sense of touch is implied through the mention of them kissing in the book's second verse.

In the same verse, both taste and smell are implicit. It is said that their love is more delightful than wine. The drinking of wine, suggested here, involves the beverage's aroma (smell) and taste.

The sense of smell again is invoked by the mention of perfume in verse three.

Sight is featured in verses five and six. In verse five, she is described as "dark...yet lovely" and her sun-darkened skin is mentioned again in verse six.

In verse seven, she includes the sense of hearing by asking him to tell her where he grazes his flock of sheep and where he rests them in mid-day heat.

"If you do not know, most beautiful of women," the shepherd says at the beginning of verse eight, "follow the tracks of the sheep and graze your young goats by the tents of the shepherds."

This reinforces the factual information that he is a shepherd and that, to him, she is beautiful.

Allegorically, I think we can take it to mean from this that, in the eyes of the Lord, people who have accepted His offer of salvation through faith in His atoning bloodshed for their sins have become beautiful. I find this comforting and amazing.

Consider: Here is the Creator of all things admiring the beauty of a human creature who He obviously loves very much. You would not think that the Almighty God who created everything by merely speaking the right words would be so attentive and caring to something He had called into existence.

This draws us back to the first book of the Bible where, after speaking things into existence, the Creator describes each of them as "good." At the end of the first day He takes inventory and decides it is all "very good." (Gen. 1:31).

In Genesis chapter two, we have a more complete description of the creation of the two human beings who, by now we know, are His favorite creatures. I find this to be both an endearing and humbling chapter of the Bible. When we become frustrated by personal sin and difficult circumstances, this is a good chapter to read because it describes God's love for us in spite of ourselves.

Satan, God's sworn enemy of the spirit world, was impressed. He began his inveterate warfare against humanity in Genesis chapter three by inducing the woman to sin, and then standing aside as she lured her husband.

At that point, the devil must have been smiling, but that was before God's great love for His human creatures became pre-eminent, even when they sinned.

Chapter one of *The Song of Songs* closes with a remarkable exchange of complements between the loving couple:

He begins this section by calling her the "most beautiful of women." (Song 1:8). Later, he adds: "How beautiful you are, my darling! Oh, how beautiful!" (Song 1:15)

To this she responds: "How handsome you are, my lover! Oh, how charming!" (Song 1:16)

Our praises for God should not be confined to a collective act in a church on Sunday mornings. What should it be like? If it still holds a place on YouTube when you read this, I suggest watching and taking part in the singing of the song "Thank you. Jesus, for the blood."

If Charity Gayle's rendition is gone from YouTube, well, then, just tell Jesus how much you love and appreciate Him and all He does. You can do that orally or silently, anytime, anywhere.

Praising Jesus, to me, is one of the highlights of being a Christian.

Song Two: Are We Ready?

Chapter two of *The Song of Songs*, like its predecessor, is powerfully sensory. Texts associated with each of the five senses appear here, just as they did in chapter one. This is because the relationship between the two lovers, although deepening, still is in preliminary phase. Attraction to each other is based more on sensory responses than depth of mutual understanding.

An indication of progress in their relationship appears in verse three where the beloved (believer) says this: "I delight to sit in his (the Lord's) shade, and his fruit is sweet to my taste."

This draws us, in our allegorical study, to the first two verses of Psalm 91: "He who dwells in the shelter of the Most High will rest in the shadow of the Almighty. I will say of the Lord, 'He is my refuge and my fortress, my God, in whom I trust.'"

She has come to realize, even at this early stage of their relationship, that He means much more to her than the consummation of physical appeal. He is to her a place of protection and rest, a companion who is earning her complete trust.

Oh, that we, His people, could say the same with absolute trust, no fear, no worry, no hindrance whatsoever. But as we enter the end-time, there is turbulence without and within. This is opinion, but I'll say it anyway: I do not think we are ready for all that lies ahead, even as Jesus laid it out for us in prophecy via Matthew 24, Luke 21 and Mark 13.

The first thing he mentioned in His end-time sermon was deception: "Watch out that no one deceives you." (Mat. 24:4) The caution against deception by false Christs and false prophets that he spoke of earlier already has met fulfillment.

The two most prominent predictors of Christ's return that I am aware of were popular TV personalities who sold millions of books based on false prophetic utterances. Both are proven to be false prophets by the simple fact that their prophecies were not fulfilled. For instance, the return of Jesus didn't happen in any of the 30-plus years prophesied by one of these men. The other man based his prophecy on events, four specific possibilities that he mentioned.

He was hedging his bets, hoping that he would hit home on one of the four.

All four were flops.

The Holy Spirit makes no mistakes in prophetic utterances he inspires. These appear in the Bible. Therefore, these two men were false prophets at the very first error of each. But, oddly, both retained Christian devotees long after they had been proven false.

This should not happen. But Jesus predicted it in his end-time prophecy. And, of course, He was right.

The most important issue here for us is this: Are we ready for the physically and emotionally stressful things Jesus prophesied for the end-time?

Jesus emphasized the need for preparation twice in his sermon. He said: "Therefore keep watch, because you do not know on what day your Lord will come. But understand this: If the owner of the house had known at what time of night the thief was coming, he would have kept watch and would not have let his house be broken into. So you also must be ready, because the Son of Man will come at an hour when you do not expect him." (Mat. 24:42-44)

Are we ready for Jesus to return? Or for the scary events prophesied to precede His coming.

Let's consider this segment of our commentary on *The Song of Songs* to be a tool for helping us get ready. What we need to do is watch. That is, pay attention to what is going on all around us. It will be a great help, of course, if we become able to recognize the celestial sign of His return. (Mat. 24:27-31, Luke 21:25-28)

One series of events, precipitated by the CCP virus, already has led us into perilous territory not previously ventured into during the entire history of the United States of America – not physical peril, as yet, but moral and economic jeopardy.

We need to start getting ready for what is ahead of us, especially the great tribulation (persecution) prophesied by Jesus and the phenomenal restoration and revival to follow. These will result in the salvation of many, many people. When Jesus does return, He will take back with himself to heaven one-third of earth's occupants. (Zech. 13:8-9)

We need to get emotionally prepared for any suffering we may have to endure, remembering always that whatever we suffer will be deserved because of sin. Our suffering will not be as severe as that endured by our Savior, Jesus, who didn't deserve any of it.

We also need to prepare as Bible students for participating in the great final revival. That will involve much prayer and insight into how we should share the Gospel with unbelievers, should we have opportunity to do so while we still live on this earth.

The degree to which we are able to accomplish all that He desires for us to do will depend upon the depth of our trust in Him. If we ask Him in faith, He will show us all we need to know.

But the weaker our trust, the more susceptible we will be to believing false prophecy, following false Christs and incorrectly identifying the celestial sign of our Savior's return.

Song Three: Coming Attractions

This part of the story, as far as the Shulammite is concerned, is what has been called, in motion picture lingo, a feature of coming attractions. Her lover leaves inexplicably in the middle of the night, foreshadowing a second departure during what turns out to be the climax of the story. The difference is that in this first segment of the narrative, he makes a timely return, with full entourage. (Song 3:6-11)

The second and final time? We'll get to that in Song Five.

Chapter three of *The Song of Songs* opens with a sleepless night for the Shulammite. The King does not come home, and she wonders why. Finally, anxiety overcomes her and she arises while it is still night and begins walking through the city, looking for him. This, of course, is a dangerous thing for a beautiful woman to do, as she discovers unhappily the second time she tries it.

But this time her search bears fruit.

While making rounds, the city's watchmen find her. She asks them: "Have you seen the one my heart loves?"

The Bible does not say what, if any, response the watchmen made to her question. Maybe they just checked her out and liked what they saw for future reference. But shortly thereafter we read this comment by the bride:

"Scarcely had I passed them when I found the one my heart loves. I held him and would not let him go till I had brought him to my mother's house, to the room of the one who conceived me." (Song 3:1-4)

The spiritual concept depicted by the bride's determination to find and cling to the one she loves is abiding. The activity of a Christian seeking close relations with Christ involves a determination to make contact with Him and then to hold on. Another way of describing it is practicing the presence of the Lord.

Some of the spiritual highlights of believers' lives involve the sovereignty of God and His work alone. Abiding is different. The believer who desires an intimacy with the Lord on a deep spiritual level clings to Him in the same way as a loving wife to her husband. Their physical home may be called an abode. But in this story, the Lord is their spiritual residence.

Song Three is effective on two levels.

The role of the believer in the process of abiding is described by Jesus in the fifteenth chapter of the biblical book of John. The analogy involves a vine and its branches and fruit. We now quote Jesus from verses 4-10 of John 15 in the New King James Version which features the word *abide:*

"Abide in Me, and I in you. As the branch cannot bear fruit of itself, unless it abides in the vine, neither can you, unless you abide in Me. I am the vine, you are the branches. He who abides in Me, and I in him, bears much fruit; for without Me you can do nothing. If anyone does not abide in Me, he is cast out as a branch and is withered; and they gather them and throw them into the fire, and they are burned. If you abide in Me, and My words abide in you, you will ask what you desire, and it shall be done for you. By this My Father is glorified, that you bear much fruit; so you will be My disciples.

"As the Father loved Me, I also have loved you; abide in My love. If you keep My commandments, you will abide in My love. Just as I have kept My Father's commandments and abide in His love."

As implied by Jesus' words, above, efforts of a believer to obtain an abiding relationship provide opportunity for the start of a greater work by the Lord. It is He who produces the spiritual fruit and who grants positive answers to requests of abiding believers.

It is also His love that is featured in the relationship. The believer abides in that love and bears more and more good fruit.

This "fruit" may consist of improved personal character, stronger ties with the Lord, and/or the eternal salvation of others accomplished through the testimony of the strengthened one.

He wants us to abide in Him and, according to what we have just read, grants positive answers to requests by serious abiders. So, it seems that all we have to do to obtain the desired position of abiding is to continue seeking close company with Him while asking Him to grant us success in that endeavor. He is our abode.

"It is in Him that we live and move and have our being." (Acts 17:28).

Song Four: How Beautiful!

Their courtship now over, the lovers have married (Song 3:11). They may be pictured at a heavenly altar, as he speaks the words of Song chapter four to her. He starts by looking into her eyes and saying twice: "How beautiful!" These words have turned into the theme for a song by Twila Paris climaxing: "How beautiful is the body of Christ!"

And so the allegory continues. The church has long been recognized in type as the body of Christ. He heads the relationship but her devoted presence is necessary for it to work. The body cannot function without direction from the head. But the head is not effective without a body to do its will. And so it is in the Kingdom of Heaven. Jesus heads it up. Faithful believers function in various capacities. All are useful.

In this remarkable chapter, He praises just about everything about her. Has any human being, in this life, ever had a more loving spouse?

A highlight appears in verse seven: "All beautiful you are, my darling, there is no flaw in you." This refers to her heavenly status where sin has no more presence. He atoned for it all by the shedding of His purgative blood at Calvary.

In the next verse He calls her his bride for the first time, saying: "Come with me from Lebanon, my bride."

Lebanon was known in ancient times as a beautiful place with magnificent trees. He is calling her away from that to an even more beautiful environment. A wonderful thought for Christians going through trials is that we should be so blessed in the afterlife by His presence in such a place.

Toward the end of this discourse, he begins referring to her as "my sister, my bride." This, to a believer, is a reminder that the males among us are known as "brothers" and the females as "sisters." But the combination of the words *sister* and *bride* in the same context seems out of place.

It shouldn't.

To the Lord, male believers are brothers to each other and part of his collective "bride" personally. Women are sisters and members of the same spiritually-wedded relationship. It is not either; it's both.

While discussing this same subject in John chapter 3, John the Baptist said this: "The bride belongs to the bridegroom. The friend who attends the bridegroom waits and listens for him, and is full of joy when he hears the bridegroom's voice. That joy is mine and it is now complete." (John 3:27-29)

This book is about the end-time. My wife is deceased, having been taken away from the evil to come. We loved each other very much, but if I had to do it all again, I would spend a lot more time telling her everything I loved about her, as did the Lord to His bride in the text we just studied: Her physical features, her generous heart, her engaging personality, and her deep commitment to Him.

Based on the extravagant language of chapter four of *The Song of Songs*, it doesn't seem as if the Lord would mind if I exaggerated. To me, it doesn't appear that the Lord considers exaggerated loving praise to be on the same level as outright lying.

What is the anticipated reaction to such praise, at least, most of the time? Well, the response of the bride in Song chapter four was to invite him into her fragrant garden where he was to "taste its choice fruits." No matter how you read this, literally, or with overtones of lovemaking, it is obvious that her intent now is to please him.

And in the chapter that follows she will prove it beyond doubt, risking her dignity and, finally, her life in a desperate effort to find him after his mysterious disappearance.

This couple is going to be together for a long time. Correction: Make that, forever.

Song Five: The Heart of Love

Chapter five of *The Song of Songs* is one of the most intriguing parts of the Bible. As we enter early phases of the end-time, it becomes more and more important that we understand the spiritual principles of this chapter.

Up to this point, the romance between the king and his beloved Shulammite has been progressing. But, now, without warning, he makes a second unannounced departure, leaving her alone. And this time, unlike before, she cannot find him.

The scriptural account of this climactic event appears in Song 5:2-6. It is written from the perspective of the Shulammite:

"I slept but my heart was awake. Listen! My lover is knocking: 'Open to me, my sister, my darling, my dove, my

flawless one. My head is drenched with dew, my hair with the dampness of the night.'

"I have taken off my robe – must I put it on again? I have washed my feet –must I soil them again? My lover thrust his hand through the latch-opening; my heart began to pound for him.

"I arose to open for my lover, my fingers with flowing myrrh, on the handles of the lock. I opened for my lover, but my lover had left; he was gone. My heart sank at his departure. I looked for him but did not find him. I called him but he did not answer."

There are times, during the lives of Christians, when we do not feel the presence of our loving Lord. He "departs" from us, inexplicably. As the Creator of the universe and its sustaining source of power, He is able to make his presence known to us at any and all times. Why the "departure"?

It could be because of an unconfessed sin. Or, it may be a test. He wants to give us a chance to prove the depth of our love for him and our trust in Him. What it means, in this case, is interrupting sleep in the middle of the night to go on a search for someone who has left no clues. Even so, he has promised, "You will seek me and find me when you search for me with all your heart." (Jer. 29:13)

In the May, 2021 of Jonathan Cahn's newsletter, *Sapphires,* is a sermon summary relating to this topic. Cahn dealt with subject matter referring to the "holy unpresence" of Jesus. He said the Lord sometimes withdraws his tangible presence from believers in order to deepen their faith.

We have seen evidence of that *unpresence* twice in the Song of Solomon when the bridegroom suddenly and mysteriously left the bride alone. Cahn wrote: "He (Jesus) had to leave so that the disciples could learn to walk by faith, grow deeper in knowing Him and that the Spirit could then come. Sometimes, in order to know the Lord, He has to take away those things that you were relying on that you might *truly* know Him. When you feel that He's far away from you, it doesn't mean that He's not there. It's just His *unpresence*. It means He wants you to grow up, to grow stronger in faith and to grow deeper in love."

And so, in the middle of the night, without taking time to make sure she is dressed warmly and appropriately, she goes looking for him. The intensity of the search demonstrates the depth of the Shulammite's love. But the test isn't over.

While the Shulammite is searching, she is accosted by antagonistic watchmen. Perhaps they are the same ones she has encountered before. Their identity is not as important as is what they do to her: "They beat me, they bruised me, they took away my cloak, those watchmen of the walls." (Song 5:7)

If in place of the word *cloak*, we insert *nightgown*, it presents a clear picture. She was naked, or close to it. And the exposed parts of her body were badly bruised. One or two small bones may have been broken.

How did the Shulammite react to the physical and emotional pain inflicted by the watchmen, on the heels of her distress over the sudden departure of the man she loved?

She asked for help from the friends who have been hanging around since the beginning of this story. She says to them. "If you find my lover, what will you tell him? Tell him I am faint with love." (Song 5:8)

Her friends, perhaps lukewarm believers or unbelievers, are unimpressed, jealous, or both. They ask her a leading question, perhaps with some sarcasm, based on her earlier praiseful comments about the man who now has deserted her:

"How is your beloved better than others, most beautiful of women? How is your beloved better than others, that you charge us so?" (Song 5:9)

In other words: "If you are really so desirable, why did he leave you? Why should we go looking for this guy?"

The next part of the story quotes the Shulammite's amazing comments about the lover who had left her alone to be assaulted by wicked men. (Song 5:10-16) He did not come to her aid while she was being beaten. And yet her description of him is passionately praiseful.

Christian friends, how I hope that if I am ever in a situation similar to hers that I will react with as much dignity and love. She said only loving things about him and did not even say a bad word about the men who had beaten her. She concluded with these words about him in the chapter's final verse:

"His mouth is sweetness itself;
He is altogether lovely.
This is my lover, this my friend,
O daughters of Jerusalem."

Now the bride's entourage is impressed. Their attitudes change. They have become eager to help their distraught companion. They say to her, "Where has your lover gone, most beautiful of women: Which way did your lover turn, that we may look for him with you?" (Song 6:1)

I am not sure if these previously hesitant so-called friends of the bride really had been her friends. But now they are. They want to help.

This is the way it often happens in the realm of Christianity. If the Christians who are being persecuted respond with love, onlookers are so impressed that they have a change of heart. Many under circumstances like these turn their hearts and lives over to this Jesus who is beloved by those who suffer for His sake.

Paul wrote: "Everyone who wants to live a godly life in Christ Jesus will be persecuted." (2 Tim. 3:12)

Jesus said in his end-time sermon. "Then you will be handed over to be persecuted and put to death, and you will be hated in all nations because of me." (Mat. 24:9)

He said this to his disciples shortly before being crucified. He also said these other things, which are also for us: "You have heard that it was said, 'Love your neighbor and hate your enemy.' But I tell you, 'Love your enemies and pray for those who persecute you, that you may be sons of your Father in heaven." (Mat. 5:43-44)

And, "Blessed are those who are persecuted because of righteousness, for theirs is the kingdom of heaven. Blessed are you when people insult you, persecute you and falsely say all kinds of evil against you because of me. Rejoice and be glad, because great is your reward in heaven, for in the same way they persecuted the prophets who were before you." (Mat. 5:10-12)

This is true love. It is the kind of love that all of us, as members of the collective bride of Christ, should manifest under every circumstance accruing to our relationship with our Savior and Lord.

We should express loving praise for Him at every opportunity, even in circumstances where it may provoke hostility in unbelievers. This will be important during the prophesied duress of the end-time. He is worthy of our most lavish praise. He may use it for the salvation of these same unbelievers.

But first and foremost for us is a personal answer to this question: *If I were badly injured and deserted, as was the bride, could I respond with so much love?*

Song Six: Gathering Lilies

The bride now has acquired respect, even admiration. In answer to sincere questions from friends about where her lover has gone and how they can assist with the search, she assures them that she knows where he is. He has told her that he was going to his garden to gather lilies. She does not specify, but it seems likely that those lilies will be decorating her bedside as she recuperates from injuries.

She says confidently to her friends, "I am my lover's and my lover is mine." (Song 6:3) They belong to each other, intimately, like Jesus and a devoted disciple.

He must not have wasted much time in picking the flowers because the next thing we know, he has returned to her side, perhaps handing them to her. His next words to her are: "You are beautiful, my darling." (Song 6:4).

Whether we are thinking of him at this moment as King Solomon or King Jesus, it doesn't matter within an allegorical context. If the recipient of that praise is thought to be either the Shulammite or the faithful Christian disciple, this is a highlight of the king's praiseful remarks:

"Sixty queens there may be (Solomon had many, Jesus has more.), and eighty concubines, and virgins beyond number; but my dove, my perfect one, is unique." (Song 6:8-9)

In reference to our relationship with the Lord, yes, in Him, we are perfect, delivered from sin by the blood He shed for us at Calvary. And, yes, we are unique in that no other human being is exactly like any one of us.

But underlying the literal words is something else: He has been describing the sacrificially loving Shulammite as beautiful and dear to himself. Now, he seems to be boasting about her, possibly still in the presence of her friends.

Allegorically, we may consider the meaning for ourselves. Each of us is unique, as was the Shulammite. But what about the rest of the qualifications? Are we as loyal to Jesus as she was to Solomon? Are we willing to accept ridicule without saying a retaliatory word? Willing to go on solitary quest for Him? Willing to undergo persecution for His sake?

Perhaps we have become lackadaisical about our relationship with Him, as so many church members seem to have done during recent years. This scenario is described perfectly by Jesus in his critical comments about the ancient church at Laodicea. (Rev. 3:14-22)

If, as I (and many others) believe, the seven churches are prophetically dual – that is, both contemporary to John and progressive through history – then the Laodicean church, the seventh and last, represents Christendom during the final era of world history.

Appropriately, the Lord Jesus Himself spoke these words to John about that church, and He has preserved them for us:

"I know your deeds, that you are neither cold nor hot. I wish you were either one or the other! So, because you are lukewarm – neither hot nor cold – I am about to spit you out of my mouth. You say, 'I am rich. I have acquired wealth and do not need a thing.' But you do not realize that you are wretched, pitiful, poor, blind and naked. I counsel you to buy from me gold refined in the fire, so you can become rich; and white clothes to wear, so you can cover your shameful nakedness, and salve to put on your eyes, so you can see. Those whom I love I rebuke and discipline. So be earnest and repent." (Rev. 3:15-19)

Each of us should do some soul-searching. Are we among the zealous believers who are committed wholeheartedly to loving and serving the Lord who has redeemed us?

Or is our faith lukewarm?

Song Seven:

More than half of the book of *Song of Songs*, to this point, has consisted of conversation between the king and the Shulammite girl who adores him. From the allegorical perspective, in which the King is Jesus and the Shulammite represents believers who love

Him, all of this conversation can be described by a single word:

Prayer.

This prayer is different from most. In our conversations with the Lord, we have a tendency to emphasize personal requests. Whatever we think will bring good health and prosperity, i.e., happiness, to us and members of our families is a major theme. It is not, however, the focus of the allegorical ideal, which also can be described by a single word:

Praise.

If conversations between every husband and wife were anything like those of the king and the Shulammite, romantic love would so dominate the lives of married couples in this world that the word *divorce* might be eradicated from our dictionaries. Divorce attorneys would have to change their specialization.

These two lovers waste little if any time talking about themselves unless asked to do so. Their attention is focused on lauding each other.

This kind of relationship pleases God, who created one man and one woman individually for each other and then placed them together in a garden. According to His creative design, in both aspects of the present allegory, personal relationships with Him and our spouses appear to be the most important things in our adult lives.

Prayer and praise can bring fulfillment.

Details of the seventh chapter of the Song of Solomon add much to what we have said so far about the importance of praying (talking to God) and praising Him. The chapter opens with the words *How beautiful*, and these are repeated at the start of verse six. This is the fourth appearance for this meaningful phrase in the Song of Solomon. See Song 4:1, where it is mentioned twice.

The first noticeable point of interest, as the Bridegroom begins to speak lovingly to the bride, is that the newlyweds already have achieved intimacy rarely found today in a marriage. Beginning with her feet, he lauds every visible part of her and, I do mean, *every* part: legs, navel, waist, breasts, neck, eyes, nose, head, hair: "How beautiful you are and how pleasing, O love, with your delights."

Three times he mentions her breasts, leading some Bible interpreters, with limited understanding, to begin thinking of pornography instead of reproductive spiritual love. This is the kind of intense love that turns observant unbelievers into believers and believers into passionate lovers of the Lord! It will be discussed in more detail in conjunction with our commentary on the eighth and final chapter of *The Song*.

Total intimacy in marriage is a wonderful thing. Too often in our culture, there is more intimacy out of wedlock than within it. For a Christian fiction book I wrote, the most memorable line from a reviewer was this from a sarcastic critic: "Hey, those Christians actually had sex!"

It was implicit, not explicit, but, yes, the Christian couple in my book were indeed intimate with each other. That's the way it should be, and the more, the better. One of the sinful scenarios that, unfortunately, has become nationwide with encouragement from popular-but-immoral entertainers, is the sad contrast between "loving" adulterers and fighting married couples.

Immorality is not always prevalent in reality, of course, but it has been overemphasized in contemporary movies, TV news and talk shows and drama.

In the seventh chapter of *The Song*, the bridegroom and bride seem to be almost shouting out: "Let's get back to basics. We love everything about each other and that's what the Lord wants to see in those of us who are married."

The Bridegroom concludes praiseful comments for the bride. These are of such intensity that we should consider making them exemplary for our own most intimate relationships. The delighted bride then responds with this:

"I belong to my lover and his desire is for me. Come, my lover, let us go to the countryside. Let us spend the night in the villages. Let us go early to the vineyards to see if the vines have budded, if their blossoms have opened, and if the pomegranates are in bloom. There I will give you my love." (Song 7:10-12)

This was an idyllic honeymoon if ever there was one. And we receive the impression that this couple's love will increase as the years pass.

Chapter seven concludes with these words of the bride: "The mandrakes send out their fragrance, and at our door is every delicacy, both new and old, that I have stored up for you, my lover." (Song 7:13)

Mandrakes are often used to typify reproductive love.

These two newlyweds are already in such a deep relationship that, if we wanted to add here a discussion of secure salvation, we could do so. The text, however, is so powerful that it hardly seems necessary. Eternal salvation is already descriptive of this new bride, as it is for everyone who – with heart, soul, mind and strength – loves and trusts the Bridegroom, Jesus Christ.

We are reminded that all of this was founded on the basis of loving verbal communication (prayer) and admiration (praise).

Song 8: The Love of God

Most of the final chapter of *The Song of Songs* is a continuation of the praiseful dialog between lover (Jesus) and beloved (Shulammite).

In what may be considered a climactic statement for this book, she says: "Thus I have become in his eyes like one bringing contentment." (Song 8:10).

How many of us can say honestly that we believe we are so close to God, through His Son Jesus, that we bring contentment to Him? I know that if I have done this at all, it has been a rare occurrence. Even as a believer, all too often I have said and done things that I know have displeased Him.

One thing about *The Song* that has captured my attention is the reversal of attitude of the so-called friends of the new bride. At the outset of the story, they were dubiously-motivated inquisitors of hers with doubts about the man who was to become her husband.

Their doubts disappeared after she went looking for him. She was beaten for his sake by watchmen and left injured and half-naked in the tattered remains of her undergarments. Instead of self-pity, she expressed love. And now her so-called "friends" really are. They are actually more than friends. They are admirers.

This is a reminder of these words of Jesus: "Blessed are you when people insult you, persecute you and falsely say all kinds of evil against you because of me. Rejoice and be glad, because great is your reward in heaven." (Mat. 5:11-12a)

Instead of cursing those watchmen, her first reaction after being left bloody and bruised was concern for her new husband. Where was he? Had something happened to him?

Her feelings for him were so ardent and sincere that the "friends" were won over. Their doubts disappeared. They volunteered to help her look for him. (Song 6:1)

Now, in chapter eight, we learn the outcome of this search. Not only are the lovers reunited, but the friends have been fully captivated by their love. We find out that the friends are sisters – that is, allegorically, Christian "believers" – and they have a younger sister whom they love.

In a dramatic reversal from earlier in the story when the bride was asking them for help, they tell the Shulammite:

> "We have a young sister
> And her breasts are not yet grown.
> What shall we do for our sister
> For the day she is spoken for?"
> —Song 8: 8

The sarcasm is gone. Now, the sisters are trying to follow the loving example of their newlywed friend. Their reversal is completed by a new concern: Not only have they been impressed to the point of personal repentance, but they want to know what they can do to protect their little sister. They think the new bride, who has reacted to persecution with love, may be able to help them.

This appears to be a permanent conversion by the bride's friends. It has been accomplished not by a memorized gospel presentation by the bride on behalf of her husband, but by the testimony of her overpowering love.

In her the friends see such an extraordinary love for her new husband (allegorically, Jesus) that they want to experience the same kind of redemptive relationship and to assist their little sister in so doing.

This is not to say that verbal gospel presentations are unimportant. Many persons have been drawn into relationship with Jesus by hearing the scriptures accurately quoted. But, sometimes, it is the person making the presentation – the testimony of personal character and love – that leads directly to a conversion.

Yes, we do need to be able to share from scriptures the salvation process that is so beautifully summarized in Romans 3:23-24: "All (human beings) have sinned and fall short of the glory of God, and are justified freely by his grace through the redemption that came by Christ Jesus."

If scripture is underlined by a personal life dominated by love and faith, this can present a powerful combination.

The love and joy of the bride in the *Song of Songs* is possible for all believers at all times, because of God's ever-presence. He loves all of us at once. We can identify with the Shulammite woman and her friends.

His last words to her were these: "Let me hear your voice." (Song 8:13) With billions of devotees, you might think the Lord of the universe would be unable to distinguish individual voices amid the cacophony crying out to Him. Not only does the request to hear the bride's voice refute this idea, but it shows that He wants us to talk to him as much as possible, that He will listen, and even that He enjoys hearing our supplications.

He wants us to pray.

In response, she says, "Come away with me." It is her desire to spend a lot of time with Him, loving each other and engaging in conversation. This is precisely what He wants from each of us, our persistent loving presence. The King and the bride have reached the point in their relationship where He would have all believers to be with Him.

In this book we have wandered from the original end-time theme involving devious politicization, But the deviation is not without reason for it is evident that the U.S.A. right now is involved in spiritual warfare as described by Paul in the sixth chapter of his letter to the Ephesian believers.

Spiritual warfare is executed successfully not on the field of battle but in the backrooms of prayer. The commanding general of America's near-miraculous victory in the Revolutionary War was George Washington. The most noteworthy characteristic of Washington was his commitment to pray for two hours every morning, with much of that time being spent uncomfortably on his knees.

Like Washington, we need to acquire as much knowledge as we can about our personal situations. Like him, we must use all of the weapons of spiritual warfare at our disposal. And like him, having received guidance from the Lord, we must be obedient.

Sincere love and strong personal character, such as that displayed at the end by all of the main characters in *Song of Songs*, is essential for our success.

Many end-time details are found in the biblical chapters of Matthew 24, Mark 13 and Luke 21. Yes, it looks bad, but we are nowhere near the joyful conclusion. At that time, each of us who believes that Jesus suffered, bled and died to cleanse us from sin will experience a Holy Spirit-propelled launch into heavenly spheres.

For those who have been experiencing upper levels of marital intimacy on this earth, like King Solomon and the lovely Shulammite, the heavenly transition will be a smooth one.

FINAL WORD

THEMES FOR END-TIME LIFE

Always based on Scripture, the first seven chapters of this book and each of the eight chapters of *Song of Songs* have primary themes. These are relevant for life at any time, but we can anticipate their importance escalating as we move into and through the time of the end. That era will not close until the moment of Jesus' Second Coming.

These, based on the text of this book, are the themes that are important to us as we prepare our hearts for whatever may happen between now and the end:

1. Watch objectively for cultural crises.
2. Attune watchfulness to biblical ethics.
3. Talk (pray) to God about everything.
4. Add this to prayer: Prepare and share.
5. Stand firm no matter what: Fear not.
6. Be God-centered, not self-centered.
7. Always trust the trustworthy Savior.
8. Love Jesus with our entire being.

9. Recognize the sky-sign of His return.
10. Abide with Him and receive His love.
11. Tell your lover details of your love.
12. Pray and praise God amid persecution.
13. Learn: Is my faith fervent or lukewarm?
14. Obtain fulfillment in prayer and praise.
15. God's Love, Salvation & Contentment.

Every one of these things is based on spiritual – ethical and/or moral – principles. Even the apparent objectivity of a careful watch (No. 1) should be based upon what is being sought. Are we looking for personal advantage or for the welfare of others? We should watch out for our own well-being, of course, but should not ignore anyone else in the line of fire.

The scriptural phrase "watch and pray" is basic and will become even more important during prophesied end-time calamities and persecutions (Nos. 2 & 3). Jesus spoke more about prayer than anything else, but his end-time sermon reiterated the need for watchfulness most often, especially watchfulness for the celestial sign heralding his Second Coming (Mat. 24:27-31). This is because, in order to act as Jesus directed, we will need to know what is going on. Fortunately, we will not be alone in this task. The invited Holy Spirit will be our guide.

Prepare and share is an evangelism plan (No. 4). Since we have been told by Jesus that multitudes upon multitudes will be saved during the time period between tribulation and His return, it is important for us to prepare, that is, to learn how to share the gospel of salvation. Testimony of Christ's love for us personally may be as important or, in some cases, even more important than the formula for trusting and asking him to forgive our sins and lead us heavenward. If something wonderful has happened to us through our Christian faith, unsaved listeners will realize something just as good could happen to them if they repent and trust Christ.

Jesus used the phrase *stand firm* during his end-time discourse because some of the things he was prophesying were scary (No. 5). Fear is a deterrent to righteous living. To this he added the suggestion that we avoid the related pitfalls of worry and anxiety (Luke 21:14, 34). Jesus said, "Come to me, all who labor and are heavy laden, and I will give you rest." (Mat. 11:28)

I have heard it preached that the seat of all sin is the self (No. 6). Richard Wurmbrand wrote this about self-centeredness: "Solomon's Song belongs to those who have made the greatest renunciation of all: the renunciation of themselves."[4]

The hundreds of self-based words in the dictionary have been mentioned, but what can we do about our sin-center? Jesus answered that question with these words: *Watch and pray*. Every time we detect sin, we should ask God for forgiveness and strength to withstand future temptation.

---

[4] Wurmbrand, *The Sweetest Song*, p. 11.

Trusting the trustworthy should be a principle that explains itself (No. 7). But there are times when we need to remind ourselves of what Jesus has done for us, especially our eternal salvation. We can recognize occasions when our trust is not fully upon Him by the answer to one simple question: Are we afraid or worried about anything? Fear and worry are signs of faltering trust.

In *Song of Songs*, the Shulammite's love for the king who allegorically represents Jesus is so intimate and intense that, merely by remaining in her presence, her "friends" are turned from sarcastic observers to believers exercising that faith on behalf of their youngest sibling. We cannot love Jesus too much (No. 8). Talking to Him (prayer) and reading His word (the Bible) are basics, but, if possible, we should not sever communications with Him at all. Whatever happens at any time may be committed immediately to Him through praise, thanksgiving, spiritual songs and unselfish requests.

Besides this book, I have written several others about the end-time, including two for the purpose of identifying the celestial sign Jesus said would herald his return (Mat. 24:30). Reasons for my conclusion are to be found in those books: *The High Sign* and *Day of the Lord* (No. 9). It is worth reiterating that there are more than 200 points of evidence that the sign will be a great comet, and not a single thing I have found that contradicts this conclusion.

The verb *abide* is related to the noun *abode*. An abode is a physical dwelling place. But in the figurative language of the Bible, it is a spiritual one. The closeness of our relationship with God may be ascertained through spiritual discernment (No. 10), If we are in an abiding state, the Lord will remain in our thoughts much of the time. Those thoughts will translate into extended times of praise, supplication and thanksgiving. He will never be far from our spirit and its outreaches into body and mind.

A memorable thing to me about my study of *Song of Songs* was the candor of the conversation. As God's allegorical representative, the king held nothing back, praising every part of his bride's body from feet to hair (No. 11). She, as the believers' representative in the story, was equally praiseful of everything that she loved about him. This is an ideal, but those of us who are married, engaged or, even if we have a boyfriend or girlfriend whom we sincerely love, should take a chance: We should speak out and tell our beloved exactly how we feel. I know a man who lost a girl he loved because he didn't have the courage to tell her how much he loved her and why. But, even if this is just about God and us, we should talk to Him about our love for Him.

Jesus prophesied that during the end-time we (Christians) will be hated in all nations, that is, worldwide, and this hatred will lead to persecution (Mat. 24:9). It will be a great test for us. We will pray. But will we trust God enough to be praiseful of Him?

Or will we do more worrying and complaining than praising and thanking? Though the answer to these questions may seem simple right now, it may not be so easy if and when suffering becomes intense (No. 12)

The answers to the hypothetical questions posed in the preceding paragraph should lead to correct conclusions concerning question No. 13. Whichever is dominant in our prayers – praise and thanksgiving, or worrying and complaining – probably will give us the correct answer as to whether our faith is fervent or lukewarm. And what is the solution for lukewarmness? We should resolve to praise and thank God even if the situation appears bleak. He will do whatever He knows to be the right thing, even if we do not understand it.

Here are those key words again: prayer and praise (No. 14).They have appeared so often in this summary of important themes for end-time living that they must be at or near the top of the list, as far as God is concerned. So let's talk to Him with conversation that includes many interjections of praise and thanks. He has said of thanksgiving that we should find something to be thankful about in every circumstance (1 Thes. 5:18). If we emphasize praise and thanksgiving in our conversations with the Lord, personal fulfillment will take care of itself.

In the finality of things, God always prevails. Christians, His people, will encounter rough patches along the way, including persecution and consequential suffering. But, as long as we cling faithfully to Him,